T0128104

Your Friend,
Math

DANIEL WEIR

authorHOUSE®

AuthorHouse™
1663 Liberty Drive
Bloomington, IN 47403
www.authorhouse.com
Phone: 1 (800) 839-8640

Published by AuthorHouse 05/25/2018

ISBN: 978-1-5462-3678-8 (sc)
ISBN: 978-1-5462-3677-1 (e)

Library of Congress Control Number: 2018904420

For my Mom and Dad, whom I miss terribly and will always love.

CONTENTS

INTRODUCTION

This is a book about mathematics, a subject that people tend to avoid. Indeed, there is a concept—"math anxiety"—that first appeared around 1972 and since then, has become a major source of concern in the pedagogic (teaching) profession.

This book hopes to help readers overcome math anxiety and make math interesting and entertaining by breaking down math into convenient, easy-to-digest chapters without all the details, equations, theorems and so forth that weigh down your average high school or college math textbook. Also, there's a bit of the history of mathematics that tries to answer the question, "Why did math evolve the way it did?" Such an approach adds perspective, and has proven to be effective in gaining an understanding of math.

Towards the end, this book does get into some of the more complicated and esoteric areas of math but the way it is structured, you build up to these sections in a relaxed, conversational manner, with an understanding of these more advanced topics that does not overwhelm and get bogged down into the mathematical minutiae that more often than not confuses rather than illuminates.

So, let's begin!

0—SAVED BY ZERO

Amazingly, the ancient societies in the so-called "Cradle of Civilization" that stretched from northern Africa through the Middle East and the Mediterranean and southern Europe—as significant as their mathematical and engineering achievements were—did not have a way to symbolically represent zero. One may be flip and say that there's no use worrying about nothing, but as we go along here you will soon recognize the importance of zero in mathematical development— perhaps the most significant development in mathematical history.

Consider the numbering system of an advanced civilization of that era, the Romans. Everyone is familiar with Roman numerals: I (1), V (5), X (10), L (50), C (100), D (500) and M (1,000). But try multiplying LII by CCCIV; it's nearly impossible and admittedly, I never learned how. Even adding two simple numbers, say, 13 (XIII) and 18 (XVIII) is rather tricky. You have to write out the combined number (XIIIXVIII), place the X's together (XXIIIVIII), combine the six I's into VI, place this next to the existing V to make VVI, combine the two V's into X to make XI and, finally, stick this next to the two X's to make XXXI (31). Our decimal numbering system is much easier—you merely add 3 to 8 to get 11, keep the rightmost 1 in the ones column and carry the other 1 into the tens column and add that to the two 1's already there to make 3 in the tens column—and there's your answer (31). And this add-and-carry technique can be applied repeatedly for very large numbers, or long lists of numbers.

As cumbersome as the Roman numeral system was, it did serve many purposes, including keeping time. Indeed, the Julian calendar—implemented by decree by Roman emperor Julius Caesar in 48 BC—was quite accurate for its day, with its twelve months, 365 days, and an extra day for leap years (years divisible by 4). Roman numerals were important in astronomical observations, financial recordkeeping, government, construction and engineering, and other aspects of civilization. But as a way of advancing mathematical thought, science and technology in general, Roman numerals were woefully inadequate. We could say that the Romans didn't have a symbol for zero because it really wasn't necessary; their mathematical approaches simply weren't sophisticated enough to warrant it. Allow me to borrow a rather salient quote from a book written by math historian Clifford Pickover in 2009 (appropriately titled *The Math Book* and attributed to mathematician Hossein Arsham): "The lack of [zero] is one of the serious drawbacks of the Roman numeral system." We could add that the admittedly clumsy nature of Roman numerals is another big drawback compared to our modern 10-digit numbering system.

Even before the Romans, societies that used decimal or 10-based numbering systems had to properly position the digits in their numbers to facilitate computations. Early on, mathematicians and scribes would simply put spaces or placeholder symbols in digits that weren't 1 through 9; this was rather inefficient and eventually, between 600 and 700, civilizations in places as diverse as India and South America developed a symbol that represented a missing digit. This symbol became zero (0) over time and mathematicians in the Middle East and elsewhere began treating 0 just like any other digit, using it in numerical and algebraic computations and spreading this technique across the civilized world.

This was revolutionary. Now, with 0, there were 10 digits in the decimal numbering system; 0 made it much easier to manipulate large numbers, small numbers, or large groups of numbers in complex calculations. We can think of 0 as a digit placeholder and it is, but there's so much more to it than that. Treating 0 like any other digit greatly advanced mathematics after around 1200, leading to algebra, logarithms, calculus and other mathematical disciplines, and the advanced technology we enjoy (or at least tolerate) today. Far from being nothing, 0 was a vitally important quantity that advanced mathematics, technology, and human society and helped create our modern world.

1—BEYOND THE BEYOND

The concept of *infinity*—increasing forever without bound—probably evolved during the 17th and 18th centuries in Europe and elsewhere, as mathematicians and scientists began contemplating things like the origin and nature of the universe, the relationship between time and space, the laws of motion, the evolution of species, and similar concepts. The idea of increasing without bound kept creeping up in their mathematical analyses, and eventually a symbol (∞) was invented as a shorthand symbol for infinity.

Unlike 0, ∞ is not a number. It cannot be used in mathematical calculations; expressions such as $\frac{1}{\infty}$, $\sqrt[\infty]{x}$, 1^{∞} and so forth are meaningless. Think of ∞ as a quick, symbolic, convenient way of saying "increasing forever without bound" in a mathematical expression that is itself a collection of symbols arranged in a logical pattern (we'll go over this technique in later chapters). There is no relationship between 0 and ∞, despite the temptation to say, for instance, that $0 = \frac{1}{\infty}$ or that $\infty = \frac{1}{0}$. The latter is forbidden in mathematics; it's like asking how many times you have to put nothing into a bottle in order to fill it, which is a ridiculous question. The former is meaningless because again, $\frac{1}{\infty}$ is not a legitimate mathematical expression.

Like ∞, there is another symbol that is used in mathematical expressions but is not an actual number like 0. It's called the *infinitesimal* and means "getting smaller and smaller without bound but not getting to 0." The infinitesimal is written several ways, including the lowercase Greek letters delta (δ) or epsilon (ε) or even (and this is where some confusion might arise) our infamous $\frac{1}{\infty}$. Just like ∞, the infinitesimal is symbolic shorthand for a concept that is vitally important in mathematics and is employed in mathematical expressions, but is not used in actual calculations. We can think of ∞ and the infinitesimal as complimentary; one gets bigger and bigger and the other gets smaller and smaller, but both are used as tools to analyze mathematical phenomena in very similar ways.

Admittedly, wrapping our arms around the idea of increasing forever, or getting smaller and smaller but never reaching 0, is a challenge. But the more we use math, the easier such abstract ideas become. It's like anything else in life: Practice it, own it, make it your friend, and you'll get it. Sometimes, boiling down abstract mathematical concepts into just a couple of words helps—as in "infinitely large," "infinite number," and "infinitesimally small." Comparing and contrasting helps too, as in figuring out how 0, ∞ and the infinitesimal play out in the grand mathematical scheme of things—for example, realizing which is a true number and which isn't; which can be used in numerical computations and which can't; and so on.

2—WHY IS PI?

The Greek letter pi (π) is the ratio of the circumference of a circle to its diameter. In Clifford Pickover's *The Math Book*, we have this somewhat startling observation about π: "The most famous ratio in mathematics is π, on Earth **and probably for any advanced civilization in the universe** [emphasis added]."

π is an irrational number; in other words, it cannot be expressed as a ratio of integers, no matter how large the integers are. This means that the decimal equivalent for π goes on forever, with no pattern to the digits. To 20 decimal places, π is equal to 3.14159265358979323846. The great mathematician Archimedes of ancient Greece could have been the first to recognize this; around 250 BC, he determined that π lay somewhere between $\frac{223}{71}$ and $\frac{22}{7}$, the latter fraction most likely an approximation to π that had been used for centuries up to that time. Indeed, the fraction $\frac{22}{7}$ is an astoundingly accurate estimate for π; calculated to four decimal places (3.1429), it misses the actual value of π (3.1416) by only 0.04 percent.

Let's look at this a little closer. Suppose you were designing an impenetrable wall made up of cylindrical logs arranged vertically, and you knew that the circumference of each log was 110 inches. Using this tiny bit of information, amazingly enough, you can very accurately compute the length of the trough required to support your wall with just a few rudimentary calculations.

First, you divide 110 by 22 to get 5, then multiply this by 7 to obtain the diameter of each log (35 inches). Assuming you want your wall to be made up of 800 logs, this means that the total length of the wall trough will be 800 × 35 or 28,000 inches (2333⅓ feet). Using the generally-accepted, modern-day calculator approximation to π that goes out to 9 digits (3.141592654), we come up with a perimeter length for the wall trough of just over 2334¼ feet, which is a mere **11 inches longer** than our earlier calculation! This is a dramatic illustration of the accuracy of the fraction $\frac{22}{7}$ for π and is a big reason why the ancient civilizations were able to engineer, design and construct such elaborate and amazing infrastructure.

Beyond geometry, π pops up in mathematics seemingly just about everywhere—in probability and statistics; calculus; number theory—you name it. As an intriguing example, you can equate π to simple fractions (though it takes an infinite number of these fractions to do so); around 1500, mathematicians came up with the following formula for computing π: $\pi = 4\left(1 - \frac{1}{3} + \frac{1}{5} - \frac{1}{7} + \frac{1}{9} - \frac{1}{11} + \cdots\right)$. This enabled quick and easy calculations of π to any degree of accuracy. You could say that π makes math—and the whole world—go round. Without it, mathematics, civilization and perhaps life itself would be impossible.

Besides π, there is another well-known mathematical ratio, and it's a relatively simple concept. First, consider a line segment broken up into two sections of lengths a and b, where b is longer than a. The length of the line segment will be (a + b) and if the ratio of this length to the longer section b is equal to the ratio of b to the shorter section a, then this ratio is the *golden ratio*, the *golden mean*, or the *golden section* and is often designated by the Greek letter phi (Φ). We can get a clearer picture of this, and actually calculate the value of this golden ratio, by employing some basic mathematical analysis. Putting the above definition into equation form yields:

$$\frac{a + b}{b} = \frac{b}{a}$$

This is the same as

$$\frac{a}{b} + 1 = \frac{b}{a}$$

Letting $\Phi = \frac{b}{a}$ results in

$$\frac{1}{\Phi} = \Phi - 1$$

which is the same as

$$1 = \Phi^2 - \Phi$$

or

$$\Phi^2 - \Phi - 1 = 0$$

which is a quadratic equation of the form $ax^2 + bx + c = 0$ that can be quickly

solved using the quadratic formula $x = \frac{-b \pm \sqrt{b^2 - 4ac}}{2a}$, where a is 1 and b and c are – 1.

Doing so yields:

$$\Phi = \frac{-(-1) \pm \sqrt{(-1)^2 - 4 \times 1 \times (-1)}}{2 \times 1} = \frac{1 \pm \sqrt{1 + 4}}{2} = \frac{1 + \sqrt{5}}{2} \text{ or } \frac{1 - \sqrt{5}}{2}$$

If you pull out your calculator, you come up with Φ equal to either 1.618033989 or

–0.618033989 and since a negative value doesn't make much sense for a ratio, we

just throw it out and keep the first value. As you might have guessed, our golden

ratio, like π, is an irrational number. But its significance in nature and religion

cannot be overstated. Consider a rectangle where the ratio of the long side to the

short side is equal to the golden ratio; this is the "golden rectangle" and if you cut

out a square from this rectangle with the side equal to the rectangle's short side, the

remaining smaller rectangle will itself be a golden rectangle. Repeating this process

with smaller and smaller golden rectangles will eventually converge on what is

called the "Eye of God"; this was considered a divine symbol in the Middle Ages and

the early European Enlightenment, around 1500 to 1600.

What's more, if you trace out 90-degree circular arcs in the cut out squares such that

they form a continuous, smooth curve, you will come up with what is called a

logarithmic spiral, a geometric form that occurs again and again in nature, science

and technology (seashells, the human inner-ear cochlea, communications antennas,

etc.). Just like π, the golden ratio has this uncanny characteristic of melding diverse

and disparate areas of math into a common thread of logic, beauty and simplicity.

And here's a rather fun play on the golden ratio: We can express this ratio as an infinite number of continuing fractions, like this:

$$\frac{1}{\Phi} = \cfrac{1}{1+\cfrac{1}{1+\cfrac{1}{1+\cfrac{1}{1+\cfrac{1}{1+\frac{1}{1+\cdots}}}}}}$$

Taking this five levels deep (and being extremely careful), we come up with

$$\frac{1}{\Phi} = \cfrac{1}{1+\cfrac{1}{1+\cfrac{1}{1+\cfrac{1}{1+\frac{1}{1+1}}}}} = \cfrac{1}{1+\cfrac{1}{1+\cfrac{1}{1+\cfrac{1}{1+\frac{1}{2}}}}}$$

$$= \cfrac{1}{1+\cfrac{1}{1+\cfrac{1}{1+\frac{2}{3}}}} = \cfrac{1}{1+\cfrac{1}{1+\frac{3}{5}}} = \cfrac{1}{1+\frac{5}{8}} = \cfrac{1}{\frac{13}{8}} = \frac{8}{13}$$

$$\Phi = \frac{13}{8} = 1.625$$

which is just 0.43 percent off the actual value of the golden ratio obtained using the quadratic-equation method. At first glance, this infinite continued fraction approach seems a bit strange but if you think about it, it's just the mathematical equivalent to our repeated golden rectangle scenario on the previous page. This marriage of math and geometry would prove vital to the advancement of math in the 16th and 17th centuries, forming the basis for analytic geometry and calculus (there's a lot more to say about that later on).

4—SUMMING IT UP

If you're interested enough in math to be reading this book, no doubt you feel you're pretty handy with a calculator, and if someone asked you to add up the first 37 integers on your device, no doubt you'd take up the challenge. The problem is, we're all human. We make mistakes, especially with mundane, repetitive tasks; we get bored and / or distracted, we lose count, we have to start over and perhaps make the same mistakes again. Adding up 37 consecutive numbers is no easy task and to be perfectly honest, I seriously doubt I could do it, even with a calculator.

Is there an easier way? Yes, there is. As in the previous chapter, we have to think about this problem algebraically. To start, we can define a quantity S that is the sum of the first n integers:

$$S = 1 + 2 + 3 + \cdots + (n - 2) + (n - 1) + n$$

Using the commutative and associative laws of addition, we can also write the following:

$$S = n + (n - 1) + (n - 2) \ldots + 3 + 2 + 1$$

Finally, we can combine the two equations above by adding up the terms to the left and the right of the equals sign to arrive at

$$2S = (1 + n) + [2 + (n - 1)] + [3 + (n - 2)] + \cdots + [(n - 2) + 3] + [(n - 1) + 2]$$
$$+ (n + 1)$$

which simplifies to

$$2S = (n + 1) + (n + 1) + (n + 1) + \cdots + (n + 1) + (n + 1) + (n + 1)$$

11

and we see there are exactly n terms of $(n+1)$ on the right of the equals sign which means that

$$2S = n(n + 1)$$

or

$$S = \frac{n(n + 1)}{2}$$

Here, then, is an amazingly simple formula for calculating the sum of the first n integers, no matter how many integers we have. To compute the sum of integers in a range, say, from 21 to 69, we use this formula twice: first, to compute the sum of the integers up to 69, then the sum up to 20; we subtract the latter from the former and voila!—we have our answer. And this can be expanded to more complicated summation computations but the main thing to remember is that with this simple and elegant formula, we are liberated from the tedium and drudgery of adding up lots of numbers. Hopefully, at this point, you're beginning to get the idea of the power and elegance of math.

But what about things that can't be so easily determined? Even here, there are specific mathematical rules that govern seemingly random events. In the next chapter, we'll lay out a simple, but very infuriating, example of this.

5—LET'S MAKE A DEAL

Suppose you're on the long-running TV game show "Let's Make A Deal." You get picked for the next deal and you're given the choice of three doors. Behind one of the doors is a brand-new car; behind the other two are goats—a brown goat and a white goat. You pick a door, hoping you'll win the car but realizing that the odds are that you'll get either the brown or the white goat. You realize that for any door, there are three outcomes: you get the car, the white goat, or the brown goat.

But then, the emcee says, "You can keep the door you picked or you can switch to another door." To sweeten the deal, the host says he'll open one of the unselected doors to reveal either the white or the brown goat, after you've made your choice to keep your door or switch. So what do you do?

At first blush, it doesn't seem to matter. If you keep your original door and the host opens another door with a goat, you have a choice between the car and the other goat—a 50 percent chance to win the car. If you switch, you have the same situation. Or do you?

Let's go back to the very beginning, which is the first cardinal rule for solving tricky mathematical problems. When you first select a door, as mentioned earlier, you have three possible outcomes: you either picked the car, the white goat, or the brown goat. Now suppose you took up the host's offer and switched to another door. Here's where you need to think very carefully and methodically:

On your original pick, if you selected the door with the car behind it (a one-third probability), if you switched to another door, you'll get a goat. It won't matter what the host does after that.

If you originally selected the door with the white goat behind it and you switched as the host opened up the other door, you'll win the car because the other door will have the brown goat.

If you originally selected the door with the brown goat behind it and you switched, the host will open up the door with the white goat behind it and again, you win the car.

So we have three scenarios that involve switching to another door; two of these win you the car, so if you switch doors, you have a 2 / 3 probability of getting the car compared to 1 / 2 if you keep the door you originally selected. It takes a bit of thinking and analysis to realize this, but it does work (it's been proven experimentally on the science reality TV series "Mythbusters").

But why is this so? What changes between keeping your original door and switching to another door? The answer is a well-known theorem in probability and statistics called Bayes' Theorem; this essentially says that given an initial event, if you add conditions (switching to another door; revealing a third door) you change the probability of the outcome from what it would have been otherwise. In physics, we see the same thing with the Heisenberg Uncertainty Principle—measuring a physical quantity changes the quantity itself, affecting the measurement.

Thinking through all this, you might get the impression that the world is chaotic, random, unordered, falling apart—or as the late comedian Robin Williams said in the early 1980s, "entropying." But that grim assessment cannot be further from the truth. So-called "randomness" has very specific, defined, strict mathematical rules, just like geometry, algebra and calculus. We can lay out these rules using things like Bayes' Theorem, and even the Heisenberg Uncertainty Principle, and treat them just like we do other mathematical concepts. In the next chapter, we'll take a look at a very well known "random" device and in the process give an insight into how gamblers in Las Vegas and elsewhere keep on winning.

6—LITTLE JOE FROM KOKOMO

Anyone who's shot crap knows that expression, the origins of which are lost in antiquity. But experienced crap players know their game; they know how the dice roll to a certain number, and they have a pretty good idea what number will come up next. That's how they keep winning.

For a simple but very effective random number generator, you can't beat a pair of "fair" (non-loaded) dice. Toss such a pair of dice and you'll come up with a number ranging between 2 ("snake eyes") and 12 ("boxcars"). Each number is the sum of the numbers that come up on one die—1, 2, 3, 4, 5 or 6. Therefore, the possible combinations you can roll with a pair of dice are:

1 and 1 for a total of 2 (1 possible combination)

2 and 1 or 1 and 2 for a total of 3 (2 possible combinations)

1 and 3, 2 and 2 or 3 and 1 for a total of 4 (3 possible combinations)

1 and 4, 2 and 3, 3 and 2 or 4 and 1 for a total of 5 (4 possible combinations)

1 and 5, 2 and 4, 3 and 3, 4 and 2 or 5 and 1 for a total of 6 (5 possible combinations)

1 and 6, 2 and 5, 3 and 4, 4 and 3, 5 and 2 or 6 and 1 for a total of 7 (6 possible combinations)

2 and 6, 3 and 5, 4 and 4, 5 and 3 or 6 and 2 for a total of 8 (5 possible combinations)

3 and 6, 4 and 5, 5 and 4 or 6 and 3 for a total of 9 (4 possible combinations)

4 and 6, 5 and 5 or 6 and 4 for a total of 10 (3 possible combinations)

5 and 6 or 6 and 5 for a total of 11 (2 possible combinations)

6 and 6 for a total of 12 (1 possible combination).

The total number of possible combinations is the sum of all these outcomes—

1+2+3+4+5+6+5+4+3+2+1 or 36. Your best odds are to roll a 7 (6 out of 36

outcomes or just under a 17 percent chance); your worst are to roll snake eyes or

boxcars (1 out of 36 or just under 3 percent). If you add up all the probabilities of

getting any combination of dice, you come up with 100 percent (or 1 as the

mathematicians prefer). There is, in the mathematical parlance, the concept of the

probability distribution function or PDF—this helps determine the probability of

rolling a specific number for the two dice, or the probability of rolling less or more

then a certain number, or the probability of rolling between two numbers. This is

what experienced dice players know intuitively.

Far from being chaotic, all this follows very defined, orderly mathematical concepts.

The first, as mentioned earlier, is that the sum total of the probabilities of all the

possible outcomes is 1 (100 percent). The second is that the PDF is symmetric; in

other words, if we graphed out the probabilities of hitting each number for the pair

of dice—2 through 12—the resulting plot would show a mirror image on either side

of the peak probability value for the number 7 (0.167 or just under 17 percent). The

third is that the probability of rolling a number in a range of possible numbers (from

3 to 7, or 2 to 6, and so on) is the sum of the probabilities of rolling any number in

that range (3,4,5,6,7; 2,3,4,5,6, etc.). Assuming this range starts with 2 and

progresses to subsequent number ranges (2; 2,3; 2,3,4; 2,3,4,5; etc.), we have what

is called the *cumulative distribution function* (CDF) and if you plotted out the CDF for each number from 2 to 12, you'll generate a function that starts out at the lowest probability (less than 3 percent for "snake eyes") and ends up at 100 percent for "boxcars"—because it's certain that you'll roll a number between 2 and 12.

Finally, there's an important concept that helps frame all this into a coherent, logical scenario, and it's what's called the *expected value, mean* or *average.* This quantity merely answers the question, "Given a pair of fair dice, what is the most likely number to come up?" The answer is obvious—it's 7, because that is the number that has the most possible combinations (1,6; 2,5; 3,4; 4,3; 5,2; 6,1 for a total of 6).

In your classes, no doubt you took exams; some students in the class did very well, others not so well. The instructor might have given out the average test score for the whole class by adding up the exam scores and dividing by the number of students in the class. After some thought, you realize this is exactly what happens with our pair of dice. The class average is, conceptually, the same as the expected value (average) number that is most likely to come up on the dice (7). The one big difference here is that the dice—and by extension the expected value—don't change over time but our class average might. The teacher, realizing the class average is too high or too low, might alter the next exam to get the average closer to the school's accepted level of academic achievement. You could say this is the pedagogic equivalent of the Heisenberg Uncertainty Principle.

In the previous two chapters we dealt with basic demonstrations of two major branches of mathematics, namely probability and statistics. These branches are essentially two sides of the same coin, namely, the idea of "randomness" (and again, that's a rather unfortunate term in math) and the rules governing it. In the last two chapters, we covered situations with a limited number of outcomes—three in our "Let's Make A Deal" scenario and 36 for our pair of dice. In real life, we can put together a situation where the number of possible outcomes is tiny—two, perhaps—but the *sample size*, the number of events (tries) to reach these outcomes is enormous, maybe even in the tens or hundreds of millions.

The most obvious way to visualize this is that old tried-and-true experiment of flipping a coin and noting whether it comes up "heads" or "tails." But no one has time to flip a coin a hundred million times, and it would be impossible to get one hundred million people to all flip their coins at the same time. There has to be another way to conceptualize this and there is, and it comes from the world of politics.

In any election at any level (local, state, national), you usually have to choose between two candidates, the Republican or the Democrat. Occasionally, an independent, non-affiliated or minor-party candidate will be lucky enough to be one of the top choices but the bottom line here is that we're trying to emulate our coin-flipping example with a real-life scenario. Think of Candidate A as "heads" and Candidate B as "tails." When Election Day rolls around and hopefully everyone gets to the polls, that's like having our one hundred million coin flippers doing their thing simultaneously.

Now here's where the probability and statistics come in. Before Election Day, there are numerous polls that ask potential voters whom they might vote for—Candidate A or Candidate B. Just like trying to get millions of people to flip coins at the same time, however, it is impossible to ask *every* potential voter their preference; there could be millions of such individuals and a survey of that size would take far too long, cost too much money, and be a waste of time. Pollsters, therefore, used what is called a *random sample* (there's that unfortunate word—*random*—again!). This random sample, which is much smaller than the pool of potential voters, is selected to mimic that pool of voters. In other words, a poll that samples 1,000 eligible voters might try to predict the winner of a Presidential election where 125 million voters turn out on Election Day.

But how can that be? How can 1,000 people surveyed at random say who's going to be the next President in an election where tens or hundreds of millions of votes are cast? It seems impossible, but as was shown previously, there are specific rules in probability and statistics that can help us estimate an overall outcome, even with a relatively tiny sample size. Just as we can estimate that most likely, rolling a pair of dice will yield a 7—or a number close to 7—we can make a prediction, an educated guess if you will, as to who will be elected President using only a tiny fraction of the electorate.

The methods for doing this involve the concepts in probability and statistics discussed previously—namely, expected values, PDFs, CDFs and ranges for a given sample size that approximate those for a large sample size. It all comes down to modeling, as accurately as possible, a massive sample size with a much smaller, more manageable sample size. Think, again, about our coin-flipping example. If you flip a coin a hundred, perhaps a thousand times and record the number of occurrences of "heads" or "tails," you might see "heads" 48 percent of the time and "tails" 52 percent. If you repeated your coin-flipping experiment, perhaps with a different coin and number of flips, it might come up 53 percent "heads" and 47 percent "tails." Ideally, you would expect your coin to come up "heads" 50 percent of the time, likewise for "tails." If you somehow had the time to flip your coin millions of times, you would indeed see it get extremely close to 50-50. This is the general idea behind polling surveys with selected, relatively small sample sizes.

There is one more idea we need to cover here, and it's a term that comes up over and over again in the media. It's another one of those annoying mathematical misnomers—the "margin of error" in a given pre-election poll. "Margin of error" seems to imply that the survey was taken incorrectly, or the statistical calculations were somehow messed up, or that the wrong sample size was used. A more accurate term is "margin of uncertainty" (MOU). Go back to the flipping-coin example; notice the difference between the ideal outcome (50-50) and the observed outcomes (48-52 or 53-47). The observed outcomes are pretty close, but there is that small variation of a few percentage points either way compared to the ideal outcome. That is the *inherent, statistical* MOU between our small sample size and the actual, gigantic sample size. It has nothing whatsoever to do with the integrity and accuracy of the sampling process; indeed, there are well-established methods for determining the MOU for a survey sample size that is much less than the actual sample size. Moreover, the MOU can be reduced by increasing the sample size, but as always, time and money constrain how big that sample size can be.

We hear it all the time: "Your vote counts." That sounds like public-service announcement pap, but mathematically, it's a very sound piece of advice. Think back to the last chapter and the margin of uncertainty. Most polls have an MOU of plus or minus 3 or 4 percent, which means that the best scenario for Candidate A in a given poll is that A's support is 8 percentage points higher than B's compared to the headline numbers (A up 4, B down 4), and at worst, A is 8 percentage points lower than B by the same amount compared to the headline numbers (A down 4, B up 4). In other words, if the headline numbers have Candidate A at 55 percent and Candidate B at 45 percent, at maximum, A could be at 59 percent support and B could be at 41 percent, for a margin of 18 percent (a blowout); at minimum, A could be at 51 percent and B could be at 49 percent, a two-point margin—basically a tossup. This is quite a swing across the MOU for our hypothetical poll, and it's one reason why voting is imperative. Statistically, you really don't know what is going to happen—who is really going to win—until all the votes are counted on election night. You might have a vague idea, but it's really just an educated guess.

To drive this point home, we can go over the 2016 Presidential election, but in a nonpartisan, logical, unemotional, mathematical way. We all recall what happened: On Election Day, November 8, 2016, Donald Trump—the GOP Presidential nominee—got more electoral votes than the Democratic Presidential nominee, Hillary Clinton, and became the 45th President of the United States. However,

Clinton received three million more popular votes than Trump, and this disparity between the Electoral College tally and the popular vote tally was the greatest since 1876. Yet that did not matter. Trump got the majority of electoral votes—306 compared to 232 for Clinton, which made him President. This electoral-college victory was secured when Trump won the popular vote in the states of Michigan, Pennsylvania and Wisconsin; his total margin of victory in these three states was just under 80,000 votes. You could say that these votes wiped out Clinton's 3-million-plus popular vote margin; 80,000 votes out of over 130 million cast works out to roughly six votes per 10,000.

Go back to 2000. That was much closer. George W. Bush won the electoral college vote by 271 over 267 for Al Gore; Bush achieved this by getting Florida's rich electoral vote prize with a 537-vote margin in that state's popular vote (everyone recalls the white-knuckle events after Election Day that year—the repeated Florida recounts; "hanging chads"; legal challenges that went all the way to the Supreme Court which eventually ruled in favor of Bush; and so on). Out of roughly 120 million votes cast nationwide that year, that comes to **seven votes out of 1,562,500**!

Finally, if you can find it, get a copy of the 2008 political thriller *Swing Vote*. Starring Kevin Costner and Madeline Carroll, this involves an excruciatingly close Presidential election where the final Electoral College tally depends on New Mexico's five electoral votes and the popular vote between the Republican and

Democratic candidates for President in that state is tied. It all comes down to Bud Johnson (played by Costner), an apathetic couch potato who doesn't give a whit about politics, and his daughter Molly (played by Carroll) who does. Molly goes to the polls on Election Day to cast her father's vote. There is a technical glitch, and the vote is not counted. After Election Day, an investigation is launched and it is determined that the vote cast by Molly for her dad is the deciding one for the Enchanted State's electoral votes—and the next President. The climax builds; Bud is wooed by both candidates and is given a do-over vote after a globally broadcast "Final Debate" between the two candidates and at the end of the movie, Bud walks into the voting booth, closes the curtain, and casts his ballot. The movie ends there; we never find out whom Bud voted for.

Of course, *Swing Vote* is an extreme example, but combined with 2016 and 2000, it illustrates a very important idea in probability and statistics. It's called regression or reversion to the mean, and it says that given a very large sample space and a very limited number of outcomes, each outcome will in the end have an equal chance of happening. Think back to the coin-flipping example. The more flips you make, the closer you will get to the ideal 50-50 scenario—"heads" half the time, "tails" half the time. So it goes with elections (Candidate A versus Candidate B). It's up to the candidates themselves to convince a very large group of people that they're the one for the job, to tilt the odds in their favor. Not an easy task, but a very good learning experience for people who want to serve in public office.

And a very good object lesson for voters everywhere. Your vote **really does count**. Yes, pay attention to the polls before the election, but recall the MOU and regression to the mean concepts—even the most accurate, trustworthy, dependable poll has that built-in uncertainty factor; every election, mathematically, is a tossup. Play it smart, beat the odds, and make a difference ... **vote**.

To paraphrase iconic broadcaster Edward R. Murrow from the 1950s: Good night, good luck, and good voting!

Before our detour into probability and statistics (and hopefully it was a useful diversion), we touched on several algebraic expressions—things like "$ax^2 + bx + c = 0$," "$S = \frac{n(n+1)}{2}$," and so forth. Algebra has been around for a very, very long time, dating back well before 1000, and if you think about it, is the natural extension of letting 0 be just like any other number. Algebra takes this concept one step further, making a letter—a *variable*—represent a number whose exact value we don't know yet. That number could be 0; it could be π; it could be an integer, an irrational number, a fraction—you name it. We just don't know it yet, and we use it symbolically as we do our mathematical analyses and calculations to arrive at our answer.

From roughly 800 to 1200, during an intellectual blossoming in the ancient Islamic regions of the Middle East, the development of algebra ("al-jabr" in Arabic) moved mathematics—and analytical or critical thinking in general—ahead at warp speed compared to earlier eras. Mathematicians such as Al-Khwarizmi, Thabit ibn Qurra, Al-Uqlidisi, Al-Samawal and Omar Khayyam laid the algebraic foundations for the earth-shaking discoveries yet to come (analytic geometry, calculus, modern science and technology), establishing algebraic rules, notations, principles and theorems including exponential notation ("raising to a power"); arithmetical manipulation of algebraic expressions involving variables; roots or "radicals"; algebraic factoring;

solutions of linear, quadratic, cubic and higher-order equations; basic statistical

concepts such as the sums of squares of integers; and so on.

Concerning analytic geometry, which we'll cover in greater detail later on, it was

Khayyam who may have been the first to embrace the revolutionary idea of

marrying algebra and geometry to solve complex and tricky mathematical problems.

Using conic sections—curves generated by slicing cones with planes oriented at

various angles yielding either a circle, a parabola, a hyperbola or an ellipse—

Khayyam was able to obtain numerical solutions to high-order algebraic equations

in a single variable, such as $ax^3 + bx^2 + cx + d = 0$ or $x^5 + x = a$; Khayyam's

methods were remarkably similar to the approximation methods used on

calculators and computers to solve these types of equations today (Newton's

method, partitioning, etc.).

Al-Uqlidisi, presaging concepts such as logarithms and numerical approximations to

equation solutions and irrational numbers, formalized the decimal (Hindu-Arabic)

numbering system into what we recognize today, with each number position

representing a power of 10 (100 or 10^2; 1000 or 10^3; and so forth) and the decimal

point marking the fractional part of the number where the number positions to the

right of the decimal point represent negative powers of 10 (0.01 or 10^{-2}, and so on).

This enabled Khayyam and mathematicians later on to present their results in a

universally accepted, easy to understand format, accelerating the advancement of math across the globe and laying the foundation for our modern technological civilization today.

In essence, then, the ancient Islamic mathematicians melded three seemingly disparate fields of mathematics—geometry, algebra and numerical representation—into a seamless, elegant, powerful, all-encompassing intellectual discipline that was light years ahead of previous mathematical discoveries. That is not to denigrate the accomplishments of the ancient civilizations that came before; delving a bit into ancient history, the Babylonian, Greek, Judaic and Roman civilizations paved the way for the Islamic mathematical renaissance by establishing the foundations of civilization—namely writing, recordkeeping, timekeeping, government, democracy, commerce, transportation, infrastructure, monotheism, law and morality.

Getting back to algebra, in the next chapter, we'll detail that most famous algebraic derivation, the solution of the quadratic equation.

10—TWO ANSWERS AT THE SAME TIME

For the quadratic (sometimes called the "second degree") equation

$$ax^2 + bx + c = 0$$

the idea is to isolate, that is "solve for," x. In other words, we want a rule or *function* of x (our unknown variable) in terms of the coefficients a, b and c, which are known. We write this mathematically as

$$x = f(a, b, c)$$

and we can think of a, b and c as inputs for our function and x as the output (engineers call this the "black box" approach; you put things in, push the button and voila!—out pops what you're looking for, namely, the value of x that satisfies the quadratic equation above). But as we'll see, there is not *one*, but *two*, values for x that satisfy this equation.

To reiterate: We want to isolate x in the above equation, and that means collecting as many terms on the right side of the equals sign as possible. We can start out thusly:

$$ax^2 + bx = -c$$

$$x^2 + \frac{b}{a}x = -\frac{c}{a}$$

and the question is, what comes next? There are still two expressions (called *monomials* or *terms*) with x in them on the left side of our equation; our goal is to only have one. For the next step, we call on Omar Khayyam, who in addition to his work with high-order equations, conic sections and so on, came up with the

30

binomial theorem which gives the formula for computing powers of binomials, namely, $(p + q)^n$. For any value of n, the resulting expression will have $n + 1$ terms. Setting $n = 2$ gives

$$(p + q)^2 = (p + q)(p + q) = p^2 + 2pq + q^2$$

and the next step is to convert

$$x^2 + \frac{b}{a}x$$

into the form $p^2 + 2pq + q^2$; this is called *completing the square*, since the result can be expressed as a square. To do this, we let

$$p = x$$

and

$$q = \frac{b}{2a}$$

Here, $q^2 = \left(\frac{b}{2a}\right)^2 = \frac{b^2}{4a^2}$ and if we add this to $x^2 + \frac{b}{a}x$ to get

$$x^2 + \frac{b}{a}x + \frac{b^2}{4a^2}$$

we see that

$$x^2 + \frac{b}{a}x + \frac{b^2}{4a^2} = \left(x + \frac{b}{2a}\right)^2$$

which is what we want (you can work out the square on the right side to verify that it is indeed equal to the left side). So now, we can proceed with solving our quadratic equation. We add $\frac{b^2}{4a^2}$ to both sides of $x^2 + \frac{b}{a}x = -\frac{c}{a}$ to get

$$x^2 + \frac{b}{a}x + \frac{b^2}{4a^2} = -\frac{c}{a} + \frac{b^2}{4a^2}$$

or

$$\left(x + \frac{b}{2a}\right)^2 = -\frac{c}{a} + \frac{b^2}{4a^2}$$

and at last, we're getting to where we need to be. We've got x isolated on the left side. The remaining steps follow naturally, keeping in mind that when we take the square root of both sides, we must account for the fact that every square root has two answers, one positive and one negative—for instance, the square root of 4 is both 2 and –2, usually written ±2. Going forward, we have

$$x + \frac{b}{2a} = \pm\sqrt{-\frac{c}{a} + \frac{b^2}{4a^2}}$$

$$x = -\frac{b}{2a} \pm \sqrt{-\frac{c}{a} + \frac{b^2}{4a^2}} = -\frac{b}{2a} \pm \sqrt{-\frac{4ac}{4a^2} + \frac{b^2}{4a^2}} = -\frac{b}{2a} \pm \sqrt{\frac{b^2}{4a^2} - \frac{4ac}{4a^2}}$$

$$x = -\frac{b}{2a} \pm \frac{\sqrt{b^2 - 4ac}}{\sqrt{4a^2}} = -\frac{b}{2a} \pm \frac{\sqrt{b^2 - 4ac}}{2a}$$

Finally, we have

$$x = \frac{-b \pm \sqrt{b^2 - 4ac}}{2a}$$

which is our solution to the quadratic equation (it cannot be simplified or manipulated further).

Going back to Chapter 3 and our quadratic equation solution to the golden ratio problem, even though we had our two answers, we had to discard one because it was negative, and a negative ratio doesn't make sense. No doubt the ancient Islamic mathematicians ran into similar real-world conundrums in their development of algebra, which required a sort of philosophical approach to mathematical analysis (and it's not surprising that these great mathematical thinkers were great philosophers and poets, too). But by the 13th century, the great mathematical strides up to that point were speeding up societal and technological change all across the globe. Ways had to be found to incorporate this new mathematics, especially Al-Uqlidisi's standardized decimal numbering system (see the previous chapter), into computational devices that could handle these new and revolutionary concepts quickly, easily and efficiently. Probably the earliest of these devices was the *abacus*, discussed in the next chapter.

The abacus first appeared in the Far East around 1200 or so. It may have been inspired by earlier decimal numbering devices, such as those used by the ancient South American Inca civilizations dating back to around 3000 BC. The ancient Incas constructed numerical recording devices called quipus ("kee-poos"); these were cords with strings and knots that were tied together to form a numerical information databank, much like computers and databases today. This information included calendar dates, construction plans, historical accounts, demographic and census data, and holiday rituals. On the quipus, numbers were represented much like the decimal system from Al-Uqlidisi's time to the present day, with groups of knots representing successive powers of 10.

But the quipus were "static"—that is, they couldn't be changed once the information was recorded. They could not be used for ongoing, real-time calculations. The abacus, which started as rows of beans or beads in grooves but eventually evolved into beads threaded onto wires mounted on a frame, *was* capable of rapid, accurate and successive computations; in essence, it was the first *digital* computer as opposed to the *analog* computer which compared like quantities (the most famous analog computer is the slide rule, which will be examined more closely in coming chapters).

On the abacus, numbers are represented as they are in the decimal numbering system. Each column of beads on a wire represents one digit (0 through 9); to save space and to make the abacus easier to handle, instead of having 10 beads per wire, the beads are broken up into an upper and lower section. The lower section has five beads, and the upper section has two beads, each representing five lower beads. To enter a number like 1,437, you would start from the leftmost column in the abacus and move up one bead in the lower section, then go to the next column and move up four in the lower section. You would then go to the next column and move up three beads in the lower section and finally, you would go to the next and last column and move up one bead in the upper section and two beads in the lower section (5 + 2 = 7).

If you think about it, this is a lot like a modern day computer's RAM (random access memory). The abacus is temporarily storing the number 1,437 for later use in computations; for example, to add 1,211 to 1,437 on the abacus, you would move up one bead in the lower section in the leftmost column to make 2. Then, you would go to the lower section of the next column, move all the beads back down, and move one bead up in the upper section and one bead up in the lower section (5 + 1 = 6). Next, you would go to the next column and move one bead up in the lower section to make 4 and finally, you would move to the last column and move one bead up in the lower section to make 3; you already have 5 in the upper section, giving you 8 (5 + 3 = 8). Your answer, then, is 2,648.

The interesting thing here is that the original number (1,437) is sequentially overwritten by the new number to be added (1,211), to obtain the answer, 2,648. This is exactly how modern computers work—except they don't do it by tens or fives; they do it using binary digits (0,1). There will be more on that later on.

With the abacus, and the very skilled operators who could perform lightning-speed numerical computations on it, mathematics expanded from the theoretical and philosophical approach of the ancient Islamic culture to a more practical application—much like the ancient Greeks with geometry and the Romans with timekeeping, government and infrastructure. The concept of the *floating-point number*—a decimal fraction where the decimal point could be positioned anywhere as the computation progressed—was a very important consequence of the abacus. Indeed, it laid the groundwork for the development of logarithms and the slide rule, and governs the computational algorithms of computers, software, networks and even social media today.

But for now, it's time to take a voyage across the seven seas, with mathematics guiding us the whole way.

12—SAILING, SAILING …

Much has been said about sailors over the millennia, not all of it complimentary. From Sinbad to Popeye to Gilligan and the Skipper and singer Jimmy Buffett, sailors have been portrayed as hardworking, dedicated lovers of the sea—and occasionally bumbling, womanizing, bar-brawling party animals ("any port in a storm"). Yet sailors and navigators were, and are, serious adherents to mathematical concepts and principles that have stretched into the most esoteric, high-powered, abstruse areas of math including relativistic physics, space-time distortion, black holes, wormholes, and multi-dimensional analysis.

Every sailor and navigator knows about the "rhumb line," which in mathematics goes by the rather scary moniker *loxodromic spiral*. This is a curve on a spherical surface (such as the Earth) that converges at, but never reaches, two points—on Earth, these are at the magnetic North and South Poles. As you sail the ocean along this curve from your starting point to your destination, your angular compass bearing will stay constant. In other words, as you pass through successive longitudes, your bearing angle with respect to these longitudes will be the same, even as your latitude changes.

This works for one-way or round-trip voyages; for a round trip, all you need to do is get a new compass bearing and follow this new bearing back home. Mathematically, you are tracing out a new loxodromic spiral path that is different from your original path; this new path follows the old path but does not intersect it. Both paths

eventually converge at the magnetic North and South Poles.

The rhumb line was discovered by Portuguese mathematician Pedro Nunes in 1537;

32 years later, Flemish cartographer Gerardus Mercator figured out how to plot

rhumb lines as vertical straight lines on a map of the Earth with the latitude lines

represented as horizontal straight lines. This was (naturally) called the Mercator

projection map and was the motivation behind the invention of the marine

chronometer in the 18th century that enabled the accurate calculation of longitude

using celestial navigation. In 1599, English mathematician Edward Wright laid out

the analytical basis for the Mercator map; we'll get into the gory details of Wright's

analysis later on. But Wright figured out a very important aspect of math, especially

higher math—the concept of *conformal mapping*—namely, changing the shape and

characteristics of the geometric coordinate system being used to model and analyze

a mathematical concept. This type of analysis can get extremely complicated, but is

vital in the study of things such as quantum mechanics, astronomy, network theory,

group theory and other concepts that stretch the bounds of mathematical thought

and analysis to this day.

The advancement of navigational technology provided by the rhumb line and the

Mercator projection map accelerated the growth and development of regional and

global economies and societies; the resulting commerce demanded the handling of

complicated, intricate mathematical calculations. Along with the universal adaptation of Al-Uqlidisi's decimal numbering system and the development of the abacus, accountants, scribes, engineers and government officials were confronted with mathematical operations involving quantities in the thousands or millions, or with complicated fractional decimals such as the approximation to π (see Chapter 2); something had to be done to simplify these tedious calculations. For instance, try multiplying 3.141592654 by 234.6785 by hand without messing up. It's like adding up a long list of sequential integers (see Chapter 4). Inevitably mistakes will be made because again, we're all human. But in the spirit of the summation formula derived in Chapter 4, mathematicians discovered a very accurate, but elegant and simple, way to represent large and / or complicated numerical quantities in computations, which built upon the work of the ancient Islamic mathematicians centuries earlier.

13—LIKE FALLING OFF A LOG

One thing I recall from my high school math courses in the mid-1970s is an adage from my advanced algebra teacher, who said, "A logarithm is an exponent." Think back to Chapter 9 and the development of algebra; the use of exponents greatly simplified mathematical expressions and made them much easier to manipulate. For instance, if you see the expression $xxxxxxxxxxx$, you can't immediately tell what you're looking at. You have to stop and count all the x's (11) and if you're in a hurry, you might not get the right count the first time. But with exponential notation, we simply write x^{11} and immediately know we're talking about 11 x's multiplied together.

A *logarithm* to the base b of a number a is the exponent to which b is raised to obtain a. The most widely used logarithm today is the logarithm to the base 10, because it fits in neatly with the 10-digit numbering system and in mathematics, consistency is key. So we take our base 10 and raise it to the base-10 logarithm of the number— written as "$\log_{10} a$"—to get the original number; or in mathematical terms,

$$10^{\log_{10} a} = a$$

Because of the ubiquitous nature of base-10 logarithms, over the years, mathematicians have dropped the "10" subscript in the expression "$\log_{10} a$" and simply wrote it as "$\log a$." This is called the *common logarithm*, a designation designed to distinguish it from the *natural logarithm* (we'll go over natural logarithms later on).

From this, we see that the common logarithm of 1,000,000 is 6, because $10^6 =$ 1,000,000. It's easier to deal with 6 than 1,000,000, as long as we keep track of what we're dealing with. But there's a lot more to logarithms than distilling down huge numbers into smaller, easy-to-digest pieces. To illustrate this, again, we go back to Chapter 9 and the rules of algebra.

In algebra, we have the following two rules of exponentials:

$$x^m x^n = x^{m+n} \text{ (multiplication of exponentials)}$$

$$\frac{x^m}{x^n} = x^{m-n} \text{ (division of exponentials)}$$

Here, we can set x to our logarithm base—10 for common logarithms—with the exponents m and n equal to the base-10 logarithms of our numbers x and y. If we apply our definition of the base-10 logarithm on the previous page to the above rules, we get

$$10^{\log x} \times 10^{\log y} = 10^{(\log x + \log y)}$$

which simplifies to

$$xy = 10^{(\log x + \log y)}$$

using the first rule. Using the second rule, we have

$$\frac{10^{\log x}}{10^{\log y}} = 10^{(\log x - \log y)}$$

which becomes

$$\frac{x}{y} = 10^{(\log x - \log y)}$$

If we wish to extract the nth root of a number x, another rule of algebra states that

$$\sqrt[n]{x} = x^{\frac{1}{n}}$$

and here, in terms of logarithms, we have

$$\sqrt[n]{x} = \left(10^{\log x}\right)^{\frac{1}{n}} = 10^{(\log x)\left(\frac{1}{n}\right)} = 10^{\left(\frac{\log x}{n}\right)}$$

Raising a number x to a power is similar:

$$x^n = \left(10^{\log x}\right)^n = 10^{(\log x)(n)} = 10^{(n\log x)}$$

So here, we have powerful calculation tools for multiplication, division, roots and powers using logarithms; seemingly impossible computations are reduced to basic math—multiplication and division are reduced to addition and subtraction of logarithms; roots and powers become multiplication and division.

Invented by Scottish mathematician John Napier in 1614, logarithms quickly became the dominant method for complex calculations for the next three and a half centuries; tables of logarithms were generated for engineers, surveyors and navigators. These tables usually had two columns made up of numbers and their corresponding logarithms; to multiply two numbers, you would look up the logarithms of both numbers, add them together, and find the result in the number column. The same went for division, except the two logarithms were subtracted. For roots, the logarithm was divided by the root index and for powers, it was multiplied by the exponent.

Less than a decade after Napier's discovery of logarithms, English mathematician William Oughtred found a way to represent logarithms graphically, as line segments on sliding pieces. Here, to multiply two numbers, you would add their lengths and look up the answer on a number scale; to divide two numbers, the lengths were subtracted. Powers and roots worked similarly; the lengths were doubled or tripled

for squares and cubes and were cut in half or thirds for square and cube roots. This

device, called the *slide rule*, was used by engineers to design everything from the

Empire State Building to the passenger jet to the Hoover Dam. Every major

scientific and engineering accomplishment by human civilization from the early

17th century to the latter half of the 20th century would not have been possible

without the slide rule, and it wasn't until the early 1970s when the slide rule would

be replaced by the electronic pocket calculator.

14—GOING NATURAL

Besides base-10 logarithms, another set of logarithms based on another number became widely used roughly a century after the development of logarithms and the slide rule. This number first appeared during the latter half of the 17th century during the development of calculus (more on that later), but it was Swiss mathematician Leonhard Euler in the early 18th century who first studied and analyzed the number extensively. This number, called e, comes up repeatedly in areas as diverse as physics, finance, electrical engineering, probability and statistics, requiring a new type of logarithm using this number as a base. This logarithm is called the "natural logarithm" and is written "ln x," an abbreviation for "logarithm natural of x." In strictly formal logarithm notation

$$\ln x = \log_e x$$

but the expression on the right is almost never used in mathematics. Like π and Φ, e is irrational; this was demonstrated by Euler in 1737. To nine decimal places, e is equal to 2.718281828.

In addition to the natural logarithm, e is used in what is called the *exponential function*, e^x. In finance, this function is used to compute continuous compound interest; it is also used in biology, in the study of how populations of species reproduce and eventually use up all the available resources. In electrical engineering, it is used in a modified form to analyze circuits with analog or digital periodic signals. It comes up repeatedly in probability and statistics, in the calculation of probability distribution and cumulative distribution functions (see

Chapter 6) for situations with very large sample sizes and myriad outcomes such as

student standardized tests scores for an entire school district.

In addition to multiplication, division, powers and roots, most slide rules were able

to calculate $\ln x$ and e^x; indeed, these two functions are related to the common

logarithm, the basis for the slide rule, in the following manner:

$$\ln x = \frac{\log x}{\log e}$$

$$e^x = 10^{(x \log e)}$$

As significant as the contributions of the abacus, rhumb line navigation, the

Mercator map, logarithms and the slide rule were to the advancement of

mathematics, science, technology and human civilization, towards the 20th century,

even more powerful and efficient means of computation were needed. This need

exploded during and after World War II, and opened up a whole new industry that

became a significant part of the American—and the global—economy.

15—BITS AND BYTES

Our digital world, love or hate it, is based on the simplest numbering system there is—the binary system, represented by the numbers 0 and 1. The importance of 0 cannot be overemphasized here; it's half the available number symbols! Every modern electronic computer made after the mid-1940s, when the Electronic Numerical Integrator And Calculator (ENIAC) was built, used and still use, the binary number system in its basic calculations.

You can think of the modern computer as an extremely huge, complicated abacus with uncounted columns of two beans each working at incomprehensible speed, and in reality, this isn't that far away from how the computer actually works. After the ENIAC was introduced in 1946, IBM produced the Selective Sequence Electronic Calculator (SSEC) in 1948. Both devices used thousands of vacuum tubes to represent binary digits—"off" for 0, "on" for 1—but the SSEC had features the ENIAC did not, namely, the ability to write programs on punch cards or punched paper tape, and provide the results on line printers. By contrast, the ENIAC had to be programmed by rewiring the vacuum-tube digital circuits. The SSEC had an Arithmetic Logic Unit (ALU), not too different from the modern microprocessor CPU; the SSEC stored programs and data on 400-pound reels of IBM card stock paper and used a programming language similar to the earliest versions of FORTRAN.

The obvious problem for the earliest computer programmers and engineers was how to represent the 10 decimal digits (0, 1, 2, 3. 4, 5, 6, 7, 8, 9) in binary format. With the ENIAC, and going through the large "batch" processing computers in the late 1960s, the method used was called Binary Coded Decimal (BCD), where each decimal digit was represented by eight bits (**b**inary dig**its**). This was called a *byte* and each byte could represent up to 256 characters (the decimal digits plus letters, special characters, signs—positive or negative—and control characters).

But this BCD scheme seemed rather inefficient; using eight bits to represent a single decimal digit was wasteful. Computer engineers compensated for this by "packing" their BCD digits—having eight bits represent *two* decimal digits, four bits per digit, with the remaining bit combinations reserved for signs, overflow and error flags. But again, this was not terribly efficient; in a string of 20 packed BCD decimal digits, there were 120 bit combinations that weren't being used for the digits. Schemes such as Excess-3 ("XS-3") were used to address this, but the challenge was clear: To represent digital numbers as bits, the bit groupings representing the numbers had to be an even power of 2 (8 bits per grouping, 16 bits, etc.).

In the binary system, each successive bit position is a power of 2 instead of a power of 10 in the decimal system, going from left to right. Thus, the binary-digit number 1110 would be, in digital (base 10) notation, $2^3 + 2^2 + 2 + 0 = 14$. Building on this, we can group our bits in threes, which would have binary numbers ranging from 000 (0) to 111 (7). Our numbers, written in this format, would go left to right in powers of 8 (512, 64, 8, etc.) and the highest digit would be 7 instead of 9 in the decimal system. This is called the *octal* numbering system and was used in many very large and powerful computers in the 1960s and 1970s. Yet even the octal system was not the most efficient numbering system for computers; after around 1975, the *hexadecimal* system came into wide use and is in just about every digital device in use today.

In the hexadecimal ("hex") numbering system, each 4-bit group pattern (0000 to 1111) is assigned a number from 0 through 9 and extending further to A for 10, B for 11, C for 12, D for 13, E for 14 and F for 15. With this system, we get maximum efficiency with the binary system because each 4-bit pattern is set to a specific digit. Hexadecimal numbers behave just like 10-based decimal numbers, grouped in powers of 16 (4096, 256, etc.). With "hex," your 8-bit byte can range from 00 to FF (in binary, 00000000 to 11111111); this represents 256 possible numbers, just as a two-digit base-10 number represents 100 numbers.

Today, we talk about a "32-bit" or a "64-bit" operating system (OS). Windows 7, for instance, is a 32-bit OS; its recent successor Windows 10 is a 64-bit OS. What this means is that in each OS, each *word*—a group of bytes used to partition binary digits in calculations—is either 4 bytes or 8 bytes long. The 8-byte word OS, because of its longer word length, can represent many more types and layers of data than the 4-byte OS. 8-byte OS systems, then, are more versatile than 4-byte systems, but require more memory and processing power due to the increased data loads from the longer word length.

On the Internet, the most common method of representing IP address—the IPv4 convention—is based on the old packed BCD technique. Each 8-bit byte of the address represents one decimal number from 0 to 255; four such groups, separated by periods, make up the address. Here, there are 4.3 billion possible addresses, not nearly enough for every device that uses the Internet. Hence the need for subnets, local area networks (LANs), either real or virtual, virtual private networks (VPNs), switches, routers, firewalls, and so on. The newer IPv6 convention for IP addresses uses 8 groups of two-byte (16-bit) words separated by colons. These words are represented by four hex numbers (0000 through FFFF); under this arrangement, there are just under 340.3 billion billion billion billion possible IP addresses— enough to power the World Wide Web for thousands of years!

Going back to the BCD era, in 1968, Hewlett-Packard—a company that heretofore made scientific measurement devices—came out with its first programmable desktop calculator, the HP 9100 A (technically, it was a computer). It did use hexadecimal in some applications such as numbering program lines, but by and large it was a BCD machine. The striking feature about this device is that it did not use a single integrated circuit. All the circuitry was constructed with discrete transistors, not unlike the ubiquitous transistor radios of the time. But a mere three years later, H-P came out with its 9800-series second-generation desktop programmable calculators, which used large-scale integrated circuits including an 8-bit-word microprocessor very similar to the processors that power every computerized electronic device today. The 9800-series processor (called the Central Processing Unit or CPU), just like the 9100, used BCD but was light years ahead of the 9100's CPU and infinitely faster. A rather shocking change in a mere 36 months!

At this point, it's time to take stock and see where we are, so in the next chapter, we'll go over the types of numbers we've looked at so far and lay the groundwork for what will come next.

16—KEEPING IT REAL

Before we delve into the main topic of this chapter, it's a good idea to review an algebraic symbolism that came about sometime after the development of algebra and greatly expanded the power and reach of algebra.

In algebra, if we have a very complicated equation or expression with lots of variables, we might literally run out of variable names since the total number of letters in the alphabet is 52, counting both lower-case and upper-case letters. We can add Greek and Hebrew letters but again, we will run out of variable names if our algebraic expressions or equations become long enough. Worse, these expressions or equations would become unwieldy and difficult to follow. To counter this, sometime after the invention of algebra in the ancient Islamic world, mathematicians began attaching *subscripts* to letter variable names—as in x_1, x_2, x_3 and so on. By doing this, mathematicians had literally an infinite number of variable names to choose from, and very complex expressions and equations could be reduced to much simpler terms.

In this algebraic scheme, each subscripted variable could be totally independent of the others, or could be *recursive*. In other words, to get from one variable to the next, you would have a mathematical formula in terms of the first variable—say x_1—whose result would equal the next variable x_2 (mathematically, this would be written as $x_2 = f(x_1)$). This formula would be applied to x_2 to get the following variable x_3 ($x_3 = f(x_2)$), meaning that x_3 would actually be a function of x_1, and so on. The subscripts themselves can be mathematical expressions; these expressions are usually limited to integer variables.

Armed with this information, we need to introduce the *general algebraic polynomial equation*

$$a_n x^n + a_{n-1} x^{n-1} + a_{n-2} x^{n-2} + a_{n-3} x^3 + a_2 x^2 + a_1 x + a_0 = 0$$

samples of which were provided previously (the quadratic equation, etc.). Just like before, the a's are the equation's coefficients. This equation is crucial in breaking down the classes of numbers we've worked with so far.

In the preceding chapters, with the exception of infinity and the infinitesimal in Chapter 2, we concentrated on specific numerical solutions to mathematical problems, either algebraically or using computational devices. Indeed, we used infinity and the infinitesimal as a contrast to actual—but very important—numbers such as π, 0 and Φ, illustrating that infinity and the infinitesimal are not true numbers, but instead are shorthand notations employed in mathematical expressions. It could be said that overall, we approached mathematics from a practical, computational standpoint—the technique that had been used by human civilization since antiquity. We shied away from the "math for math's sake" side of things, even though that concept had become rather well established by the time the ancient Islamic civilizations tackled algebra over a millennium ago.

In our presentations, the numbers we examined are collectively called *real numbers* and are broken up into four classes:

1) Integers (–3, –2, –1, 0, 1, 2, 3, and so on); there are an infinite number of integers;

2) Rational numbers such as finite decimal numbers—52.37, 0.15625, etc.; fractions such as $\frac{223}{71}$; repeating decimals such as 0.111111111 ... , which equals the fraction $\frac{1}{9}$, 0.142857142857 ... , which equals $\frac{1}{7}$, and so forth (there are an infinite number of rational numbers);

3) Irrational numbers such as π, *e*, Φ, $\sqrt{2}$, $\sqrt[3]{10}$, etc., represented by an unending, random stream of decimals (you guessed it—there are an infinite number of irrational numbers);

4) Transcendental numbers.

We haven't covered that fourth class of real numbers yet, but that's where the general algebraic polynomial equation comes in. A transcendental number is a number that can **never** be a solution of this equation, no matter how many terms you take the equation out to. In this case, the coefficients a_n, a_{n-1}, a_{n-2} and so forth *are integers or rational numbers.* The irrational numbers π and *e* are transcendental numbers. So are the logarithms of numbers that are not perfect powers of their bases; expressions such as "log 567" or "ln 169.88" are transcendental numbers. As is the case with the first three classes of real numbers, there is an infinite number of transcendental numbers. In set theory, the entire universe of real numbers is usually denoted by a script "R" surrounded by braces as in "{ℜ}."

To begin this chapter, we ask a seemingly simple question: What is the square root

of minus one? In other words, what is the solution of the algebraic polynomial

equation $x^2 + 1 = 0$? Well, in the set of real numbers—$\{\Re\}$—there is no solution.

You can't take the square root of a negative number. This is a meaningless

operation, like $\sqrt[\infty]{x}$; in the early electronic pocket calculators that came out in the

1970s, trying to take the square root of a negative number would produce a flashing

display or the word ERROR.

Yet during the 16th century, the meaning of the square root of –1 vexed

mathematicians all over Europe and the Far East. Just what was meant by this

quantity? Was it a quantity at all? Why did it keep coming up in solutions to

algebraic equations? Could it be ignored?

The ancient Islamic mathematician Al-Samawal (see Chapter 9) ran into the same

sort of quandary as he contemplated the mathematical meaning of expressions that

had heretofore been ignored or deemed unsolvable. For instance, what happened

when you took a number and raised it to the 0th power? Mathematically, what was

the expression

$$x^0$$

equal to? At first glance, it should be zero, given that exponential notation is

shorthand for repeated multiplications; x^0 should mean 0 x's multiplied together, which is 0. Or is it? This is where Al-Samawal's genius comes in. At the tender age of 19, he published a treatise titled "The Dazzling In Algebra," which laid out the infrastructure of modern algebra examined in earlier chapters. Among Al-Samawal's insights was that any number raised to the 0th power is 1, not 0. This is proved using the algebraic rule of division of exponentials (see Chapter 13) and setting the exponent of the bottom term equal to the exponent of the top term:

$$\frac{x^a}{x^b} = x^{a-b}$$

$$a = b$$

$$\frac{x^a}{x^a} = x^{a-a} = x^0 = 1$$

because any quantity divided by itself is 1.

In contrast to the practical, computational concept laid out in the previous chapters, this is the "math for math's sake" approach—an application of a very important topic in mathematics called *number theory*. Defining the 0th power of a number as 1 brings consistency, order, logic and predictability to math in general. It is not an arbitrary, off-the-cuff observation, but is a continuation of centuries of analysis (and fascination) with numbers and their properties.

Going way back to the ancient Jewish civilizations in what is now Israel, Jordan and the Palestinian territories, we find many examples of number theory; indeed, the Torah—the first five books of the Bible, also called the Hebrew Bible or the Pentateuch—has hundreds of mathematical parables based in number theory. One rather famous one is towards the end of Genesis, where Jacob gives a present of 220

goats to his brother to secure friendship with Esau. The number 220 is chosen for

its special qualities, including the fact that it can be evenly divided by many integers;

the numbers 360, 60 and 18 are similar. Beyond this, 220 has an amazing property,

namely, that the sum of all of its factors (110, 55, 44, 22, 20, 11, 10, 5, 4, 2, 1) add up

to 284, and the sum of all of 284's factors (142, 71, 4, 2, 1) add up to 220. The

number pair (220, 284) is called an *amicable number pair* and while there is an

infinite quantity of these types of numbers, only about 11 million of these numbers

have been found so far.

Given the "math for math's sake" (number theory) approach, then, how does $\sqrt{-1}$ fit

in? Could it be the base for a whole new type of number? Exactly what does it

mean? In 1545, Italian mathematician Gerolamo Cardano published his book *Ars

Magna*, an analysis of algebraic polynomial equations; here, he tried to tackle the

meaning of $\sqrt{-1}$ by using it in various calculations, combining real integers with

multiples of $\sqrt{-1}$ to obtain other real integers. This was very similar to how the

ancient civilizations treated 0—as a mere placeholder rather than an actual number.

Cardano was doing with algebra what these ancient civilizations did with 0 in their

numerical computations (see Chapter 0). Cardano was on to something, but he did

not carry it to its logical end. The true meaning of $\sqrt{-1}$ would have to wait until

others could unlock its secrets, and in so doing advance mathematics (and science

and technology) to new heights.

The first mathematician to really explore the meaning of $\sqrt{-1}$ was Italian

mathematician and engineer Rafael Bombelli, who in 1572 wrote a book titled

simply, *Algebra*. In it, he hypothesized that $\sqrt{-1}$ is the solution to the polynomial

equation—$x^2 + 1 = 0$—we introduced at the beginning of the previous chapter.

Bombelli's hypothesis was ridiculed by other mathematicians, who thought it was a

waste of time, perhaps even intellectual fraud. They branded Bombelli's analysis

"imaginary," a wild flight of fancy. But applying the "math for math's sake"

technique, why couldn't $\sqrt{-1}$ have real mathematical meaning? Wasn't it a number

just like any real number? Could it be used in numerical computations, algebraic

expressions, and other mathematical applications?

The answer to all these questions is "yes," and it was Leonhard Euler (the discoverer

of the natural-logarithm base e—see Chapter 14) who began to methodically unpack

the mysteries of $\sqrt{-1}$. He called it "i," the imaginary unit, with the property that $i^2 =$

-1. i, then, was the solution to Cardano's equation $x^2 + 1 = 0$. Euler was off to the

mathematical races; building on Cardano's work, he developed *complex numbers*,

written as $(x + yi)$, where x and y are real numbers. In the standard mathematical

nomenclature, a complex number is designated by the letter z (or, in the case of

electrical engineering, s). Mathematically, then, we can say

$$z = x + yi$$

or in the electrical engineering (EE) / control theory nomenclature

$$s = \sigma + \omega i$$

In EE, however, i represents current, so the EE's substituted j for i to eliminate confusion; their complex-number notation thus became

$$s = \sigma + \omega j$$

and truthfully, defining $\sqrt{-1}$ as j makes more sense because it says, in essence, that $\sqrt{-1}$ is a true—not "imaginary"—number and should be treated as such. For consistency and in the sprit of mathematical tradition, however, we'll use the definition $z = x + yi$ for the remainder of this book.

Going back to Chapter 10 and the quadratic equation $ax^2 + bx + c = 0$, to be mathematically precise, we need to recast it using complex numbers:

$$az^2 + bz + c = 0$$

The same solution, of course, applies, but with z instead of x:

$$z = \frac{-b \pm \sqrt{b^2 - 4ac}}{2a}$$

So for a complex-variable solution to the quadratic equation $2z^2 - 2z + 5 = 0$, we have

$$z = \frac{-(-2) \pm \sqrt{(-2)^2 - (4)(2)(5)}}{(2)(2)} = \frac{4 \pm \sqrt{4 - 40}}{4} = \frac{4 \pm \sqrt{-36}}{4} = 1 \pm \frac{\sqrt{(36)(-1)}}{4}$$

$$z = 1 \pm \frac{6\sqrt{-1}}{4} = 1 \pm 1.5i$$

$$z = 1 + 1.5i, 1 - 1.5i$$

Just as in the real-number world, our quadratic equation in the complex-number world will have two solutions, one of which will be the *complex conjugate* of the other. The conjugate of a complex number z is often written z^* and is defined as

$$z^* = x - yi$$

and we can replicate Cardano's experiments (see the previous chapter) by multiplying a complex number by its conjugate:

$$z \times z^* = (x + yi)(x - yi) = x^2 + xyi - xyi - (yi)^2 = x^2 - y^2 i^2 = x^2 - (-1)x^2$$
$$= x^2 + y^2$$

So just like Cardano did, we get a real number from two complex numbers.

Looking at our quadratic equation in terms of z, we realize that we can have functions of complex numbers just like we have with real numbers, as in az^2, $\ln z$, $\log z$ and so forth. A very significant complex-variable function is e^z, which was exhaustively analyzed by Euler. We'll cover this very important complex-variable function later on. For the moment, we'll briefly return to the heated argument over imaginary and complex numbers that consumed mathematical thought in the 16th and 17th centuries, concentrating on the actions of a very brilliant and very famous 17th century French mathematician, René Descartes.

19—GENIUS AND APOSTATE

René Descartes was a brilliant, but very independent, thinker. In 1637, he published

his treatise *La Géométrie*, which was for all intents and purposes the first modern

book on mathematics or science—something someone today (well-versed in French,

of course) could read and understand without too much effort. *La Géométrie* built

upon the work of Omar Khayyam and the other ancient Islamic mathematicians,

setting out specific rules and techniques for representing geometric forms such as

circles, parabolas, hyperbolas, lines and so forth algebraically. (An example of this is

the so-called "unit circle," a circle of radius 1, diameter 2, and circumference 2π; the

algebraic equation that represents this circle is $x^2 + y^2 = 1$.)

Ironically, Descartes was at the forefront of that group of mathematicians who

would have absolutely nothing to do with deigning the meaning of $\sqrt{-1}$. In fact, he

was the first mathematician to brand this number as "imaginary" (a term that is still

used today). This was an intellectual retaliation to all those other mathematicians

who were—in his eyes—wasting their time and intellectual energy in a fruitless

pursuit. Descartes was much more interested in advancing analytic geometry; in

addition to the work of the ancient Islamic mathematicians, he no doubt was aware

of the work of Pedro Nunes, Gerardus Mercator and Edward Wright (see Chapter

12) in analyzing rhumb lines and the Mercator map. In *La Géométrie*, Descartes was

the first to broach the concept of representing points in a plane with pairs of real

numbers; amazingly enough, however, he did not actually develop the Cartesian coordinate system, with its horizontal x axis and vertical y axis meeting at the origin, where $x = 0$ and $y = 0$.

This raises an interesting question: Was Descartes's refusal to accept $\sqrt{-1}$ a hindrance to his mathematical analyses? Had he accepted this number as a base for a new numbering system, would he have advanced mathematics beyond where it actually evolved at that time? In other words, did Descartes's anti-$\sqrt{-1}$ attitude hurt mathematical development to the detriment of future math and science discoveries?

Historically, perhaps not. Descartes's discoveries were quite earthshaking by themselves, and it was just a short time afterward when mathematicians and engineers developed the Cartesian coordinate system, building on Descartes's work. So in the end, maybe no harm was done by Descartes's refusal to accept $\sqrt{-1}$ as a legitimate mathematical entity.

All this said, Descartes's discoveries helped mathematicians, including Euler, to come up with a way of representing complex numbers geometrically. We'll have more to say about this after the next chapter. For now, we'll delve a little deeper into Cartesian coordinates, analytic geometry, and analyzing geometric shapes algebraically.

As they say, a picture's worth a thousand words; we'll include several diagrams going forward to better illustrate what we're talking about. To begin, we can plot out that very ubiquitous geometric curve, the parabola, using Cartesian coordinates:

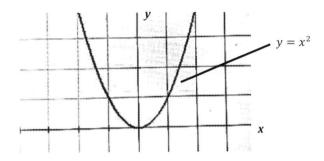

This is the graph of the function $y = x^2$ and we can find out a lot from this simple but well-known plot. To begin, we see that as we move along the x-axis, the value for y increases at a faster and faster rate; in mathematical terms, it's increasing in a *non-linear* fashion. Thinking in terms of physics, this looks an awful lot like acceleration; as we go forward in x, our corresponding y is increasing more quickly—speeding up—as if we were driving a car with our foot on the gas pedal.

Second, this plot is symmetric about the y-axis. Symmetry is a very important concept in analytic geometry because it lets us generate an entire plot with just one-half of the plot; for the other half, all we have to do is reflect our existing half-plot about a given axis called the *axis of symmetry*.

Third, our plot can be characterized by its *domain* and *range*. Domain is the

potential values of x we choose from to generate the plot; range is the resulting y-

values that result from applying the equation describing the plot (namely, $y = x^2$).

In our parabola, the domain is all the real numbers—the set $\{\Re\}$—mathematically

written as $-\infty < x < \infty$. The range is all the positive real numbers, written $0 \leq y <$

∞; this takes us all the way back to Chapter 2 and our discussion of ∞ and we see

how ∞ is applied in our analysis of the problem at hand, even though it is not

actually used in any computations. We can pick any value of x to generate a y-value;

x is therefore said to be *independent*. It follows, then, that y is *dependent*, because it

depends on the value of x chosen.

Now, using analytic (sometimes called *coordinate*) geometry, we're going to

determine the value of Φ, the golden ratio. To recap what we did in Chapter 3, we

reduced the golden-ratio equation

$$\frac{a + b}{b} = \frac{b}{a}$$

to the quadratic equation

$$x^2 - x - 1 = 0$$

where we substitute x for Φ for consistency. This equation can also be written

$$x^2 = x + 1$$

We can break this up into two functions, namely, $y_1 = x^2$ and $y_2 = x + 1$, using

subscripts to eliminate confusion. We can plot out both functions on the same

graph, like this:

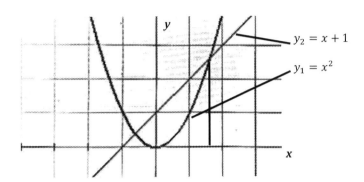

We want the x-value of the point where the two curves intersect; we aren't concerned about the y-value. This value is just over one-half of the way between 1 and 2, but not quite three-quarters. As a first estimate, we can average these distances and come up with an approximation to Φ:

$$\Phi \cong \frac{\left(1 + \frac{1}{2}\right) + \left(1 + \frac{3}{4}\right)}{2} = \frac{1.5 + 1.75}{2} = 1.625$$

which is off by just under 0.6 percent from the actual value of Φ taken out to nine decimal places (1.618033989). We can tweak our lower and upper estimates and re-do these calculations, coming up with new estimates that are closer and closer to Φ; here, we are zeroing in on the x-coordinate of the intersection point.

One interesting thing about curves in Cartesian coordinates represented by algebraic expressions is what happens when we switch variables in the expressions—for instance, if we exchange y for x in our parabola equation $y = x^2$. Doing so yields

$$x = y^2$$

or

$$y = \pm\sqrt{x}$$

taking the square root of both sides, including the plus-or-minus as we did with the quadratic formula, and placing our dependent variable y on the left side. Plotting this out, we get:

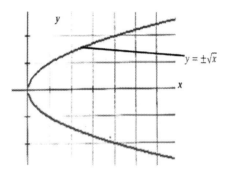

which is our parabola rotated clockwise 90 degrees, or reflected ("flipped") about a 45-degree diagonal centered at the origin and sloping upward. Like the Mercator projection map, this is an example of conformal mapping, though a rather simple one. As is the case with the parabola equation, to obtain the axis of symmetry, domain and range for this plot, we switch x and y: now the axis of symmetry is the x-axis instead of the y-axis; the domain is $0 \leq x < \infty$; and the range is $-\infty < y < \infty$.

Besides the parabola, a very important geometric curve is the unit circle, which we hinted at in the previous chapter. We'll take a closer look at the unit circle in the next chapter, and use it to delve into a critical branch of mathematics called *trigonometry.*

For the sake of argument, hopefully not—we want to talk about trigonometry (or "trig") in a general sense rather than the more restricted, numerical method used by the ancient Greeks, who invented trigonometry to determine triangle dimensions without having to actually go out and measure them, thus saving money, time and labor. The concept of trigonometry was first broached by the great mathematician Pythagoras, who developed the world-famous Pythagorean Theorem. In words, this theorem says that the sum of the squares of the horizontal and vertical sides of a right triangle is equal to the square of its hypotenuse, or in algebraic terms

$$a^2 + b^2 = c^2$$

where a is the length of the horizontal side, b is the length of the vertical side, and c is the length of the hypotenuse.

This very famous equation lays the groundwork for trigonometry; indeed, it is used to define the *sine* of the angle A measured counterclockwise from the horizontal side of our right triangle to the hypotenuse:

$$\sin A = \frac{\text{the length of the vertical or } opposite \text{ side}}{\text{the length of the hypotenuse}} = \frac{b}{\sqrt{a^2 + b^2}}$$

Then there is the *cosine* of the angle A:

$$\cos A = \frac{\text{the length of the horizontal or } adjacent \text{ side}}{\text{the length of the hypotenuse}} = \frac{a}{\sqrt{a^2 + b^2}}$$

Finally, we have the *tangent* of A defined as:

$$\tan A = \frac{\text{the length of the opposite side}}{\text{the length of the adjacent side}} = \frac{b}{a}$$

Now consider the unit circle $x^2 + y^2 = 1$; to recap, this circle has radius 1, diameter 2, and circumference 2π. If we wish to graph this circle, first we solve for y in terms of x to get

$$y = \pm\sqrt{1 - x^2}$$

and plotting this out, we get

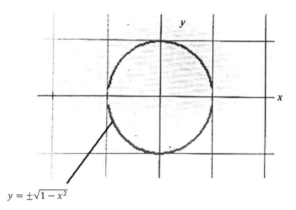

$$y = \pm\sqrt{1 - x^2}$$

Now, consider a point P on this unit circle. P will be at the apex of a right triangle with the hypotenuse going from the origin to P, with length 1. As before, we define the angle A going counterclockwise from the x-axis to the hypotenuse, corresponding to an arc length s on the unit circle from the coordinate $(x = 1, y = 0)$ to P. Putting all this together on our unit-circle plot, we get:

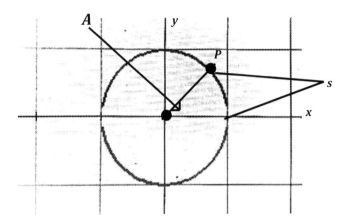

and if we let the x-coordinate of P be x_p and the y-coordinate be y_p, using our trigonometry formulas for the right triangle, we have

$$\sin A = \frac{y_p}{1} = y_p$$

$$\cos A = \frac{x_p}{1} = x_p$$

$$\tan A = \frac{y_p}{x_p}$$

The (x, y) coordinates of any point on the unit circle, then, are $(\cos A, \sin A)$. From the Pythagorean Theorem, we get one of the most well known trigonometric identities, namely

$$(\sin A)^2 + (\cos A)^2 = 1$$

or in its more standard form,

$$\sin^2 A + \cos^2 A = 1$$

Looking at the above diagram, we realize that any angle A corresponds to an arc length s. We can find the relationship between A and s using ratios; that is, we see that an angle A of 90 degrees corresponds to an arc length s of one-quarter of the unit circle's circumference 2π, or $\frac{\pi}{2}$. An angle of 360 degrees—one complete revolution around the unit circle—corresponds to $s = 2\pi$. The formula, then, to convert degree angles to arc lengths is

$$s = \frac{A}{360}(2\pi) = \frac{A\pi}{180}$$

In mathematics, these arc lengths are called *radians*, and you can think of radians as angles since they directly relate to angular degrees as measured in the unit circle. This is extremely important in mathematics, especially higher math, since radians are *dimensionless*—which means they can be incorporated into just about any mathematical equation, no matter how complicated, without fear of fouling up any unit conversions. Indeed, in standard mathematical nomenclature, when we're talking about trigonometric functions, we automatically assume that the angles (arguments) of these functions are in radians unless otherwise specified.

Finally, we need to find out how the trigonometric functions $\sin A$, $\cos A$ and $\tan A$ behave—specifically, what they look like when plotted out as functions and what their symmetries, domains and ranges are. For consistency, we treat these functions like any other function ($y = x^2$, $y = \pm\sqrt{x}$ and so on) and substitute x for A (or s), keeping in mind that x is in radians. We can then examine these trigonometric functions graphically using the same techniques as we used for our parabolas in the previous chapter.

First, let's look at the plot for $y = \sin x$. Imagining the y-coordinate of our unit-circle point as it moves around the circumference of the circle, we see that this value will start at 0 for $x = 0$ and increase until it hits its maximum value (1) at $x = \frac{\pi}{2}$. Then, it will decrease until x equals π, where it will be 0 again. It will become negative and will hit its minimum value (-1) at $x = \frac{3\pi}{2}$, and finally will move back to 0 as x approaches 2π. Afterward, this cycle will repeat itself for every interval of 2π. For negative values of x, the same thing will happen. Graphically, the function $y = \sin x$ looks like this:

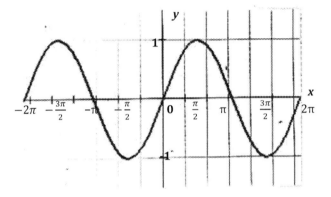

The domain of this function is $-\infty < x < \infty$; the range is $-1 < y < 1$. It is neither symmetric about the x nor y-axes.

For $y = \cos x$, the curve is similar, though it's shifted to the left by $\frac{\pi}{2}$ radians (or 90 degrees if you insist) compared to $y = \sin x$. In other words, it is *leading* $y = \sin x$ by this angular amount (EEs know a lot about this phenomenon—they call it a *phase shift* or a *phasor*). This is what $y = \cos x$ looks like:

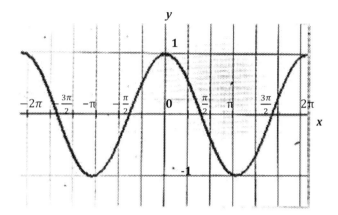

Unlike $y = \sin x$, this curve is symmetric about the y-axis (but not the x axis). Its domain and range are the same as for $y = \sin x$.

Finally, the graph for $y = \tan x$ looks like this:

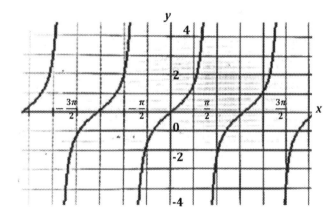

Unlike $y = \sin x$ and $y = \cos x$, $y = \tan x$ has values of x which cause it to "blow up"—more accurately, when x is an odd positive or negative integer multiple of $\frac{\pi}{2}$

$\left(-\frac{\pi}{2}, \frac{3\pi}{2}\right.$, etc.$)$, $\tan x$, which is equal to $\frac{\sin x}{\cos x}$, will result in division by zero (which is

"verboten"!) because $\cos x$ is 0 at these multiples of $\frac{\pi}{2}$. The domain of $y = \tan x$,

then, is $-\infty < x < \infty$; $x \neq \frac{n\pi}{2}$; $n = \pm 1, \pm 3, \pm 5, \dots$. The range is $-\infty < y < \infty$.

Finally, using this knowledge, we'll go back to Chapter 12 and Edward Wright's

formula for the Mercator projection map. Wright figured out how to calculate the

Cartesian coordinates x and y of a Mercator projection map coordinate defined by its

longitude l and latitude L, where x and y are in degrees and l and L are in radians and

the reference longitude l_0 (also in radians and usually the longitude at the center of

the map) is known. Here are Wright's formulas:

$$x = \frac{180(l - l_0)}{\pi}$$

$$y = \frac{180 \ln\left(\tan L + \sqrt{\tan^2 L + 1}\right)}{\pi}$$

These formulas are a very neat, concise compendium of what we've been talking

about so far in this book—it encompasses logarithms, π, trigonometry, radians and

coordinate conversions (mapping). For the moment, though, we need to briefly go

back to complex numbers and how they are represented geometrically—a

technique that will prove very important later on.

Before we go further, there is one very basic, even critical, idea in algebra that pretty much puts to rest all the skepticism about imaginary numbers that was endemic in the 16th and 17th centuries. It's called the Fundamental Theorem of Algebra (FTA), and was first proved by the great German mathematician Johann Carl Friedrich Gauss around 1800. This theorem states that there are exactly n solutions to the nth degree general algebraic polynomial equation with real coefficients

$$a_n x^n + a_{n-1} x^{n-1} + a_{n-2} x^{n-2} + a_{n-3} x^3 + a_2 x^2 + a_1 x + a_0 = 0$$

where these solutions are complex numbers—that is, with a real and an imaginary part as we defined in Chapter 18, namely

$$z = x + yi$$

A pretty important intellectual and historical load for an "imaginary" number!

But how do we actually *represent* complex numbers? We know the *real number line*, which is a line that extends infinitely to the right for positive numbers and infinitely to the left for negative numbers; this line contains the four classes of real numbers we detailed in Chapter 16—integers, rational numbers, irrational numbers and transcendental numbers. (By the way, the three trigonometric functions we explored in the last chapter, for most values of x, yield transcendental numbers.) This line, in addition to being infinitely long, is infinitely dense. In other words, no matter how close you zoom in to a portion or segment of the real number line, you will have an infinite quantity of real numbers in that segment. Yes, that's hard to grasp; we're talking about an "infinity of infinities." Probably the best way to visualize this is a one-dimensional universe where you can only go in two directions, right (increasing) or left (decreasing). Not a very hospitable universe, for mathematics or life in general.

And that's the beauty of complex numbers. We can employ the mathematical techniques of the two previous chapters and define the *complex plane*, where each complex number is a point in this plane. The horizontal axis is the *real-number axis*, and the vertical axis is the *imaginary-number axis*.

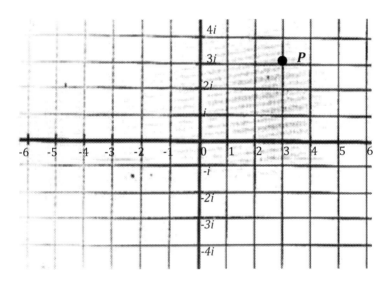

Here, the point *P* represents the complex number

$$z = 3 + 3i$$

and in the same vein as a number in the real number line, *P* is but one lowly, lonely complex-number point in an infinitely dense plane containing an infinite number of points. That said, we're in a much better situation than the real number line; as American science writer Isaac Asimov wrote in his books *Realm of Numbers* (1959) and *Realm of Algebra* (1961), going from the real number line to the complex plane was like being let out of prison and being able to wander about freely.

Looking closer at the complex plane, we could say that the horizontal and vertical axes are made up of multiples of *unit measurements*—1 for the horizontal axis and *i* for the vertical axis. This is a very important concept, and leads us to a critical field in mathematics known as *vector analysis*. To begin, we standardize our complex plane; that is, we assign unit measurements for each axis that are conceptually similar—for instance, we can assign **i** (not to be confused with the imaginary unit) to the horizontal axis and **j** to the vertical axis. In published mathematical texts such as this book, these *unit vectors* are printed in bold type to avoid confusion; in writing, we use a carat symbol above the letter (î, ĵ). Using this scheme, our complex plane becomes the *two-dimensional vector plane* shown on the next page. Here, our complex-number point *P* becomes the *vector*

$$\mathbf{p} = 3\,\mathbf{i} + 3\,\mathbf{j}$$

in printed form or

$$\vec{p} = 3\,\hat{\imath} + 3\,\hat{\jmath}$$

in written form. We plot **p** (or $\vec{p}$) on our vector plane thusly:

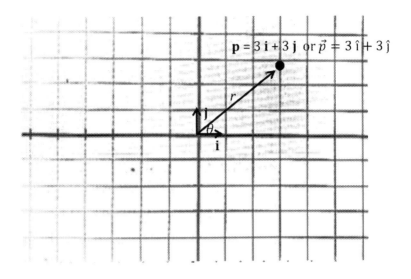

$$\mathbf{p} = 3\,\mathbf{i} + 3\,\mathbf{j} \quad \text{or} \quad \vec{p} = 3\,\hat{\imath} + 3\,\hat{\jmath}$$

We see that our vector is, along with its **i** and **j** coordinates, defined by its *magnitude* *r* and *direction* (or bearing—see Chapter 12) *angle θ*. Here, from the Pythagorean Theorem

$$r = \sqrt{p_i{}^2 + p_j{}^2}$$

where p_i is the horizontal component of **p** and p_j is the vertical component. The direction angle *θ* is

$$\theta = \tan^{-1}\left(\frac{p_j}{p_i}\right)$$

where the *inverse-tangent function* $y = \tan^{-1} x$ is obtained by exchanging x and y in the tangent function $y = \tan x$ discussed in the previous chapter; this is the same as flipping the plot for $y = \tan x$ about the 45-degree diagonal to obtain a function that has an infinite number of y-values (direction angles) for each x. The inverse-tangent function has domain $-\infty < x < \infty$ and range $-\infty < y < \infty$.

To avoid unnecessary complications, we ignore all the values of y in the inverse-tangent function that are greater than 2π (360 degrees) or less than 0. This is the standard navigator's definition of direction or bearing; this range is called the *principal* range of $y = \tan^{-1} x$. For $\theta = \frac{\pi}{2}$ (90 degrees) or $\frac{3\pi}{2}$ (270 degrees), we forego the inverse-tangent computation (because remember, it's undefined) and "hard code" the direction angle to either of these two specific values.

Just as we do with real and complex numbers, we can perform mathematical operations on vectors. We can add or subtract vectors; we can multiply vectors by *scalars*, which are real numbers; we can determine what is called the dot product or cross product of pairs of vectors (for brevity, we won't go into these operations). To add or subtract vectors, we start with the first vector **p** and from its endpoint, we add or subtract the horizontal and vertical components of the second vector (say, **q**) to arrive at the sum or difference, called the *resultant* (this term applies to either vector addition or subtraction). For addition, using vector notation, we write

$$\mathbf{s} = \mathbf{p} + \mathbf{q}$$

where **s** is the resultant vector. In terms of the horizontal and vertical components of **p** and **q**, we have

$$\mathbf{s} = (p_i + q_i)\,\mathbf{i} + \left(p_j + q_j\right)\mathbf{j}$$

with magnitude and direction angle, respectively, of

$$r = \sqrt{(p_i + q_i)^2 + \left(p_j + q_j\right)^2}$$

$$\theta = \tan^{-1}\left(\frac{p_j + q_j}{p_i + q_i}\right)$$

Subtraction works the same way. Multiplying vectors by scalars merely increases the magnitude of the vector by the scalar; the direction angle does not change. In physics, we can think of a scalar as the mass of an object and a vector as its weight; you need both mass and a gravitational force to have weight. Forces such as gravity are vectors; so are velocity, acceleration, momentum and torque. All these quantities have magnitude and direction, just as **p** does.

We need to quickly touch upon the vector components r and θ, because they serve as the basis for a very important coordinate system called the *polar coordinate system*. Going back to Chapter 12 and navigation, we can think of polar coordinates as longitudes, all originating at the North or South Pole. Another way of looking at this is to pretend we're on a stationary (geosynchronous) satellite parked over either pole. Looking down, we see all the longitude lines radiating outward from the pole (hence, *polar* coordinates) and on each line, we can mark out a distance r going towards the equator, making a direction angle θ measured from the horizontal:

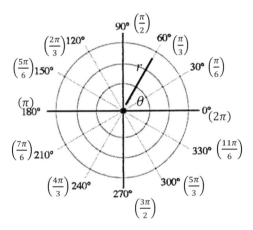

The rectangular (Cartesian) coordinates are related to the polar coordinates r, θ by

$$x = r \cos \theta$$

$$y = r \sin \theta$$

Going the other way, we can determine the polar coordinates from the x, y Cartesian rectangular coordinates:

$$r = \sqrt{x^2 + y^2}$$

$$\theta = \tan^{-1}\left(\frac{y}{x}\right)$$

which are the magnitude and direction angle of the line segment from the origin (0,0) to the Cartesian coordinate point (x, y).

At this point, we're almost through with this book, and kudos (or bravo, or *mazel tov*) to anyone who's stuck with it up to this point. The last topic we'll cover is calculus, which—despite its reputation—really isn't that terribly difficult if approached the right way, conceptually rather than being buried under reams of equations, tables, and whatnot.

Calculus was developed in the latter half of the 17th century by the great mathematician, philosopher and scientist Isaac Newton (who applied it to physics concepts such as velocity, acceleration, force and momentum), and another brilliant mathematician, Gottfried Leibniz (who developed the nomenclature in calculus that we use to this day). Calculus is the mathematics of motion, of change, and we would be hard-pressed to think of any natural or man-made phenomenon where that does not play a significant part.

Speaking of change, if we go back to our trusty parabola $y = x^2$ at the beginning of Chapter 20, we see that around $x = 0$, it's relatively flat but suddenly gets steeper and steeper as x increases. At each value of x, we find the corresponding y-value and we can estimate the slope of the curve at that point by imagining a line that is tangent—just touching—the curve at that point:

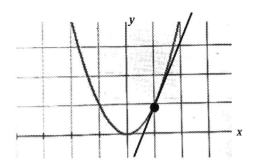

It's quickly seen that the slope of the curve at this point is $2 - \left(\frac{\text{"rise"}}{\text{"run"}}\right) = \frac{2}{1} = 2$—

double the corresponding x-value of 1; if we move to $x = 2$, we see the same thing:

the slope is 4, again twice the *x*-value. This is true for all succeeding values of *x*, and

thus we can write a slope function that describes the slope of the tangent line for all

x:

$$s(x) = 2x$$

This holds for positive as well as negative values of *x*, due to the curve's symmetry

about the *y*-axis. This slope function is called the *derivative* of the function $y = x^2$

because we *derive* it from the original function to get our slope function.

Since we take the slope at a single tangent point on the curve, we can allow our

tangent line—centered on the tangent point—to get smaller and smaller; the slope

will not change. Of course, this being a book on mathematics, we can present this

formally, using limits. We let the "run," mathematically written as Δx, approach 0;

the "rise"— Δy—will likewise approach 0. Our task, then, is to compute the slope $\frac{\Delta y}{\Delta x}$

as Δx approaches 0. Symbolically, using the limit nomenclature, this gives us our

formal definition for the derivative, which we relate back to our slope function:

$$\lim_{\Delta x \to 0} \frac{\Delta y}{\Delta x} = \frac{dy}{dx} = s(x) = 2x$$

The expression $\frac{dy}{dx}$ is the standard, most common way to indicate the derivative

because it blends in naturally with algebraic expressions. Employing this

convention, we express the derivative of $y = x^2$ thusly:

$$\frac{dy}{dx} = 2x$$

We can determine the derivative of the derivative of our original function $y = x^2$ by

plotting out the function $y_1 = 2x$ and computing the slope for all *x*. This is a straight line and immediately we see that this new slope function is

$$s_1(x) = 2$$

and this function is called the *second derivative* of our original function $y = x^2$. The

second derivative is most commonly designated as $\frac{d^2y}{dx^2}$ because, like $\frac{dy}{dx}$, it fits in

comfortably with algebraic expressions. Thus, we write

$$\frac{d^2y}{dx^2} = 2$$

where, again, $y = x^2$. Derivatives beyond the second are rarely used, even in higher

mathematics.

Instead of measuring and determining slopes of curves—which of course is

impossible if you don't have a plot of the curve handy—we apply the limit definition

of the derivative to the function itself and transform the calculation of the derivative

into a standard algebraic operation. For example, with our function $y = x^2$, we first

compute $\frac{\Delta y}{\Delta x}$:

$$y = x^2$$

$$y + \Delta y = (x + \Delta x)^2 = x^2 + 2x\Delta x + (\Delta x)^2$$

where we are adding the "rise" Δy and the "run" Δx to y and x to simulate our

infinitesimally small tangent line. Since $y = x^2$, we have

$$x^2 + \Delta y = (x + \Delta x)^2 = x^2 + 2x\Delta x + (\Delta x)^2$$

$$\Delta y = 2x\Delta x + (\Delta x)^2$$

$$\frac{\Delta y}{\Delta x} = 2x + \Delta x$$

and finally, we take the limit as Δx approaches 0, causing Δy to do the same:

$$\lim_{\Delta x \to 0} \frac{\Delta y}{\Delta x} = \frac{dy}{dx} = \lim_{\Delta x \to 0} (2x + \Delta x) = 2x + 0 = 2x$$

which is our derivative. The second derivative follows thusly:

$$y + \Delta y = 2(x + \Delta x) = 2x + 2\Delta x$$

$$2x + \Delta y = 2x + 2\Delta x$$

$$\Delta y = 2\Delta x$$

$$\lim_{\Delta x \to 0} \frac{\Delta y}{\Delta x} = \frac{d^2 y}{dx^2} = \lim_{\Delta x \to 0} \left(\frac{2\Delta x}{\Delta x}\right) = \lim_{\Delta x \to 0} (2) = 2$$

which is a constant slope.

Looking back on all this, the first derivative behaves a lot like velocity and the second derivative like acceleration. In physics, a constant acceleration will produce an increasing velocity, and that is what is happening here. Even before Newton and Leibniz, going as far back as the ancient Egyptians, Jews, Greeks and Romans, mathematicians and civil engineers were dealing with limits, velocities and accelerations, although they did not mathematically represent these phenomena. Most likely they dealt with it geometrically, similar to what we did at the beginning of this chapter.

Just as logarithmic and trigonometric functions have inverses, so do derivatives; at first, these inverse operations were called *anti-derivatives*. Later on, however, the anti-derivative revealed some rather extraordinary properties of its own and it became clear that it needed its own definitions, rules and nomenclature. It was

Leibniz who formalized the anti-derivative; he called it the *integral* and the process

of determining it *integration.* Leibniz discovered that the area under a curve—any

curve—could be computed by breaking up the region of the Cartesian coordinate

plane between the curve and the *x*-axis into infinitely thin rectangles with

infinitesimal widths and heights equal to $y(x)$, then adding up the areas of these

rectangles in a given interval of *x* to find the area under the curve in that interval.

We can mathematically represent each infinitely thin rectangle thusly:

$$\Delta A = y(x)\Delta x$$

where ΔA is the area of the rectangle. In the spirit of our discussion of the

derivative, and to be consistent, we substitute dx for Δx and dA for ΔA:

$$dA = y(x)dx$$

The terms dx and dA (as well as our previous dy) are called *differentials*—

infinitesimally small quantities that approach but do not equal 0; we can think of

them as geometric counterparts to the numbers in the infinitely dense real number

line or the points of the complex plane. The sum of all these rectangles in the

interval $a \leq x \leq b$ is written

$$\int_a^b y(x)dx$$

where the integral sign was most likely originally a stretched-out S, meaning

summation (see Chapter 4). This is called the *definite integral*, because it represents

a definite, computable quantity, namely, the area under the curve for the function

$y(x)$ between $x = a$ and $x = b$.

But before we can figure this out, we need the anti-derivative or the *indefinite integral* of our function. Unlike the definite integral, the indefinite integral is a function itself—the area function under the curve, if you will—and in calculus, there are myriad ways of finding out the indefinite integral of a function, some easy, some hideously complex. We'll focus on an easy method for doing this going forward.

If we take a simple function—say, $y = 2x$—and wish to use integration to compute the area under the curve of this function for a given interval of x, we first have to determine the indefinite integral of this function. We ask the question: What function has the derivative $2x$? We already have our answer, as we had previously worked this problem in reverse: Our desired function is $y = x^2$. But as they say in the commercials, wait, there's more. Not only does $y = x^2$ have $2x$ as its derivative; so do $y = x^2 + 1$, $y = x^2 + 100$, $y = x^2 + 1000000$—in general, $y = x^2 + C$ fits this criterion. So the indefinite integral of $y = 2x$ is $y = x^2 + C$ where C is the *constant of integration*. Generalizing this mathematically, we have

$$\int y(x)dx = A(x) + C$$

where $A(x)$ is the anti-derivative of $y(x)$.

Before we proceed further, there are two theorems of calculus we need to go over. One says that any constant within the integral sign can be taken outside; mathematically,

$$\int Ky(x)dx = K\int y(x)dx$$

which makes sense, because an integral is basically a sum and multiplying all the terms in that sum by the same number is equal to that number times the sum. Also, there is the integral rule for monomial algebraic expressions of the form ax^n:

$$\int ax^n = a \int x^n = \frac{ax^{n+1}}{n+1} + C$$

Using this rule, we come up with the indefinite integral for $y = 2x$:

$$\int 2x\,dx = 2 \int x\,dx = 2\left(\frac{x^{1+1}}{1+1}\right) + C = 2\left(\frac{x^2}{2}\right) + C = x^2 + C$$

If we only consider the function $y = x^2$, the constant of integration C will equal 0. This is called an *initial condition* or *boundary value* because we are setting the bounds for our outcome before we evaluate the indefinite integral.

Now that we have the indefinite integral for our function $y = 2x$, we can compute the definite integral for a specified interval of x, for instance, where x lies between 3 and 5. To do this, we need one more theorem from calculus:

$$\int_a^b y(x)\,dx = A(b) - A(a)$$

where $A(b)$ and $A(a)$ are our indefinite integral (anti-derivative) $A(x)$ evaluated at b and a. We calculate the area under the curve $y = 2x$ from $x = 3$ to $x = 5$ thusly:

$$\int_3^5 2x\,dx = A(5) - A(3) = 5^2 - 3^2 = 25 - 9 = 16$$

Going back to probability and statistics, which we covered in Chapters 5 through 8, we can come up with an integral expression for a very important function that was discovered by Gauss around the same time he figured out the proof to the

Fundamental Theorem of Algebra (see the previous chapter). Naturally, it's called

the *Gaussian distribution* and is expressed as

$$p(x) = \frac{1}{\sqrt{2\pi}} e^{-x^2/2}$$

where $p(x)$ is a probability distribution function (PDF) representing many possible

outcomes for a very large sample size—such as the SAT scores for all the high-

school students in a major city such as Chicago or Los Angeles. In this case, you have

potentially thousands of outcomes (the SAT scores) and millions of students in the

sample size. For this kind of situation, the Gaussian PDF is the best way to go.

For the Gaussian PDF, the domain is $-\infty < x < \infty$ and the range is $0 \leq p(x) \leq \frac{1}{\sqrt{2\pi}}$.

$\frac{1}{\sqrt{2\pi}}$ is equal to 0.3989422804, which is just over twice our peak probability value for

our pair of fair dice in Chapter 6 (0.166666667). Recall that our fair-dice PDF

peaked at the value of maximum probability and decreased from there on both sides

symmetrically; the Gaussian PDF behaves likewise. For the Gaussian PDF, we can

derive an expression for the cumulative distribution function (CDF) and before we

do this, we need to expand on our concept of the definite integral.

Previously, we assumed that the upper and lower bounds of a definite integral had

to be specific numbers. This is not so. We can use variables and we can even use

infinity (keeping in mind that this does not qualify infinity as a number). If we use a

variable, we need to define a new variable, called a *parameter*, that acts as a kind of

stand-in or temporary substitute for the actual integration variable.

For our Gaussian CDF, then, we have

$$P(x) = \frac{1}{\sqrt{2\pi}} \int_{-\infty}^{x} e^{-t^2/2} dt$$

where t takes the place of x inside the integral sign to avoid confusion. This is called

an *integral function* and is the probability that a given outcome will be less than a

specified outcome represented by x in our PDF (such as an SAT score of 1200).

To compute the probability of an outcome or range of outcomes, we use the

standard definite integral

$$\frac{1}{\sqrt{2\pi}} \int_{a}^{b} e^{-x^2/2} dx$$

where a and b are determined from our list of potential outcomes and where they

are in relation to our sample set (for instance, the range of the lowest 50 SAT scores,

or the 100 scores that group around the overall student average). Unlike our

previous integration examples, there is no neat, simple anti-derivative for the

Gaussian distribution function; it has to be calculated using infinite series or other

approximation methods.

At this point, we have just one more topic to cover. We'll explore certain types of

equations that, in contrast to the equations we've looked at previously, do not have

specific, fixed *numbers* as solutions, but *functions*.

In this chapter, we briefly discuss *differential equations.* To be honest, differential equations—"DEs" or "diff e's"—can be extremely complicated, cumbersome, laborious, and generally a pain in the rump. But the basic idea behind these types of equations is relatively straightforward.

In the previous chapter, we were actually dealing with differential equations, but in a sort of roundabout, covert way. One simple differential equation we looked at is

$$\frac{dy}{dx} = 2x$$

and our task is to find $y = y(x)$. In other words, we need to isolate y on the left side in terms of the other quantities in our equation, just like we solved the quadratic equation back in Chapter 10. We can integrate both sides and come up with an indefinite-integral solution thusly:

$$dy = 2xdx$$

$$\int dy = \int 2xdx = 2\int xdx$$

and remember, we'll have to keep track of the constant of integration in our solution. We can think of the left side as summing up an infinite number of dy's to come up with our original y; we apply the rule for integrating monomials on the right side to arrive at our solution:

$$y = 2\left(\frac{x^2}{2}\right) + C = x^2 + C$$

where, for mathematical formality, we retain that pesky constant of integration C.

As we did in the last chapter when we were evaluating the indefinite integral of $y = 2x$, we restrict our solution to a specific situation. The general solution to our differential equation, $y = x^2 + C$, describes a family of parabolas all symmetrical with the y-axis and running up and down the y-axis to positive and negative infinity. We say that we want the specific parabola described by setting the constant of integration to 0, which is of course $y = x^2$, the parabola we examined extensively in previous chapters. Just like the indefinite integral, we are applying an initial condition (boundary value); as is the case with integration, this restriction is vital in determining specific solutions to differential equations.

Probably the most famous, and well-known, differential equation is the equation that, in a branch of physics called *classical mechanics*, represents the simple harmonic oscillator (SHO). An example of an SHO is a spring connected to a bob of mass m; we wish to determine a function x in terms of time t—$x = x(t)$—where $x(t)$ is the position of the bob in relation to the rest position of the spring. At this rest position, $x(t)$ will be 0. We'll consider force, acceleration, and velocity in our analysis but to keep things simple, we won't work with vectors. We'll stick to scalars to avoid unnecessary complications.

With the spring in its rest position, the force of gravity is exactly balanced by the force of the spring pulling upward on the bob. The bob is stationary. When we pull the spring (gently!) downward and then release it, the *restoring force*—the force

pulling it towards the rest position—causes the bob to accelerate as its distance

from rest decreases. As the bob passes the rest position, it is travelling at maximum

velocity but overshoots; it then decelerates as its distance from rest increases. From

physics, we know that force equals mass times acceleration, or $F = ma$. In the last

chapter, we said that acceleration could be expressed as the second derivative of the

function we are seeking. We also see that the acceleration of the bob is the inverse,

the *negative*, of the position of the bob from the rest position. Putting this all

together, we can come up with a differential equation that describes our position

function $x(t)$ for the bob:

$$F = -kx$$

$$ma = -kx$$

$$m\frac{d^2x}{dt^2} = -kx$$

Remember, we're thinking in terms of time t instead of the x-axis value x we were

using in our previous arguments. But it's really the same thing; just as we can plot

$y(x)$ versus x, we can plot $x(t)$ versus t; we're simply using different variable names.

The value k in the above equation is called the spring constant, and can be

determined experimentally in the physics laboratory. So what is the solution to this

differential equation?

Solving differential equations is itself a bit of an art, combining luck, skill, knowledge

of the physical situation, and perseverance. For our spring-bob contraption, we

know that the bob oscillates up and down, over and over again, passing the rest point periodically. This strongly suggests either a sine or cosine characteristic for $x(t)$; it certainly isn't a tangent, exponential, or logarithm. We start observing the bob's motion—that is, the initial value of $x(t)$—when we pull the spring down and then let it go. This could be thought of as the bob's maximum position from rest at time $t = 0$, which suggests the cosine function. So, we can write our bob position function as

$$x(t) = A\cos(\omega t + \phi)$$

where the constants A, ω and Φ can be either be determined experimentally in the physics lab or estimated from the spring constant k and bob mass m. Specifically, Φ is a phase angle or phasor measured in radians—see Chapter 21—that is related to our observation interval for $x(t)$; it can be used as a reference if we're comparing several springs. *A* is the *amplitude*, the maximum displacement from rest for the bob and ω is the *angular frequency* of the bob; it is in radians per second and is related to the *periodic frequency f* thusly:

$$f = \frac{\omega}{2\pi}$$

where *f* is the number of times the bob makes a complete cycle per second (electrical engineers measure *f* in Hertz or "Hz").

This SHO analysis is for a perfect spring. But we don't live in a perfect world, and there is no such thing as a perfect spring. All springs, as they move up and down, will encounter air resistance, friction due to the stretching of the spring material that will be dissipated off as heat, and random disturbances in the spring motion. These factors will increase as the spring bob velocity increases, just like a car experiences more wind resistance going 70 miles per hour than it would going 30.

The car will also use up more gas per mile at 70 than at 30, and you could think of

this as the spring experiencing more friction, heat loss and disturbance as it hits

maximum velocity at the rest position $x(t) = 0$. The combination of these opposing

(negative) factors will be proportional to the bob velocity and can be expressed as

$$c\frac{dx}{dt}$$

where c is the spring's elasticity constant and $\frac{dx}{dt}$ is the bob velocity. Just like k, c can

be determined in the physics lab. In this situation, the bob, after it whizzes past the

rest point for the first time, won't get quite to the maximum point that the perfect

spring will on the same cycle; after it passes the rest point the second time, its

distance from rest will be smaller still, and so on. The successive peak distances

from rest for the bob will decrease with each cycle, following an *exponential decay*

function of the form e^{-x}. As $x \to \infty$, $e^{-x} \to 0$, meaning that eventually, the bob will

come to a complete stop at the rest position.

Our equation for the real-world spring and bob system, then, is

$$m\frac{d^2x}{dt^2} = -kx - c\frac{dx}{dt}$$

or

$$m\frac{d^2x}{dt^2} + c\frac{dx}{dt} + kx = 0$$

The solution to this (rather scary-looking) differential equation is

$$x(t) = Ae^{-dt}[\cos(\omega t + \phi)]$$

where d (just like A, ω and Φ) is related to k, c and the bob mass m. This is called a *decaying sinusoid* function.

Obviously, solving differential equations involves a lot of guesswork, but right around the time of Newton, Leibniz, Euler and Gauss, mathematicians came up with some rather clever techniques for estimating the function solutions to some complicated, esoteric differential equations. In these cases, we can re-cast our differential equation solution function $y = y(x)$ as a sum of an infinite number of monomial terms—an *infinite series*:

$$y(x) = A_0 + A_1x + A_2x^2 + A_3x^3 + A_4x^4 + A_5x^5 + \cdots$$

Recall that our general algebraic polynomial equation (see Chapter 16) had only a finite number of terms n, where n is the degree of the equation. Our infinite series is quite different; besides having an infinite number of terms, it must *converge*—sum up to a defined, finite, expressible function $y(x)$ that can be treated much like the functions we examined in previous chapters—functions such as e^x, $\sin x$ and $\cos x$. The coefficients must be defined recursively (we talked about that in Chapter 16); to determine $y(x)$, we plug our infinite series into the differential equation in question and find this recursive relationship between the coefficients (some of them may be zero).

In the late 18th and early-to-mid 19th centuries, mathematicians used this technique to solve the SHO differential equation as well as other differential equations, and in the process came up with some rather intriguing infinite-series

expressions for our venerable functions e^x, $\sin x$ and $\cos x$:

$$e^x = 1 + x + \frac{x^2}{2!} + \frac{x^3}{3!} + \frac{x^4}{4!} + \frac{x^5}{5!} + \frac{x^6}{6!} + \frac{x^7}{7!} + \cdots$$

$$\cos x = 1 - \frac{x^2}{2!} + \frac{x^4}{4!} - \frac{x^6}{6!} + \cdots$$

$$\sin x = x - \frac{x^3}{3!} + \frac{x^5}{5!} - \frac{x^7}{7!} + \cdots$$

where the denominators in each term in the above series are called *factorials* and

are defined as

$$n! = n(n\text{-}1)(n\text{-}2)...(2)(1)$$

Using this formula, 2! is $2 \times 1 = 2$, 3! is $3 \times 2 \times 1 = 6$, 4! is $4 \times 3 \times 2 \times 1 = 24$, and

so forth.

All this leads to a rather astonishing relationship between exponentials, trig

functions, and complex numbers. First, we let $x = z$ in the exponential function e^x

to get e^z, our complex exponential function (see Chapter 18), where $z = x + yi$:

$$e^z = e^{x+yi} = e^x e^{yi}$$

The term e^{yi}, using the infinite-series expansion for the exponential function, is

$$e^{yi} = 1 + yi + \frac{(yi)^2}{2!} + \frac{(yi)^3}{3!} + \frac{(yi)^4}{4!} + \frac{(yi)^5}{5!} + \frac{(yi)^6}{6!} + \frac{(yi)^7}{7!} + \cdots$$

and we have to determine the successive powers of i thusly: $i^2 = -1$, $i^3 = (-1) \times$

$i = -i$, $i^4 = i^2 \times i^2 = (-1)(-1) = 1$, and so on. Doing so, we get

$$e^{yi} = 1 + yi - \frac{y^2}{2!} - i\frac{y^3}{3!} + \frac{y^4}{4!} + i\frac{y^5}{5!} - \frac{y^6}{6!} - i\frac{y^7}{7!} - \cdots$$

$$e^{yi} = 1 - \frac{y^2}{2!} + \frac{y^4}{4!} - \frac{y^6}{6!} + \cdots + iy - i\frac{y^3}{3!} + i\frac{y^5}{5!} - i\frac{y^7}{7!} + \cdots$$

$$e^{yi} = 1 - \frac{y^2}{2!} + \frac{y^4}{4!} - \frac{y^6}{6!} + \cdots + i\left(y - \frac{y^3}{3!} + \frac{y^5}{5!} - \frac{y^7}{7!} + \cdots\right)$$

$$e^{yi} = \cos y + i \sin y$$

where y is in radians. Thus, we have

$$e^z = e^{x+yi} = e^x e^{yi} = e^x(\cos y + i \sin y)$$

which is called *Euler's formula*.

It is this formula which led Euler to come up with perhaps his most famous equation, which can be easily derived by letting $y = \pi$ and $x = 0$ in his formula:

$$(e^0)(e^{\pi i}) = (1)(\cos \pi + i \sin \pi) = -1 + 0 = -1$$

$$e^{\pi i} = -1$$

$$e^{\pi i} + 1 = 0$$

This one simple equation uses the four most important quantities in mathematics—e, π, i and 0—and attests to Euler's brilliance, and the brilliance, logic and coherence of math in general.

25—CONCLUSION: THE EQUATION WITH NO SOLUTION

Well, this is it: the last chapter. Here, we'll look at one last equation, a differential equation that cannot be solved but can be approximated to yield an extremely useful concept in physics (and timekeeping). Consider a pendulum of arm length l and bob with mass m (just like our SHO in the previous chapter). Here, we can ignore the mass of the bob (this is called a *simple pendulum*); we wish to derive the angular deflection x as a function of time t from the rest position, where the arm and bob are vertically stationary. We assume $x(t)$ is in radians; unlike our SHO, this $x(t)$ will move side to side rather than vertically. First, we define the distance the bob travels along the pendulum arc in terms of $x(t)$:

$$d = lx(t) = lx$$

When we pull the bob away from its rest position and release it (just like we did with the SHO), the pendulum will accelerate along this arc towards the rest position, pass it at maximum velocity, then decelerate until it reaches the other side before swinging back. In this case, the countervailing force—the force pulling the bob in the other direction—will be the component of the gravitational force g acting on the bob, which is $g \sin x$. The bob's acceleration will be the second derivative of the distance d it moves along the pendulum arc, which is $l\frac{d^2x}{dt^2}$. This yields the following differential equation:

$$l\frac{d^2x}{dt^2} = -g \sin x$$

or

$$\frac{d^2x}{dt^2} + \frac{g}{l}\sin x = 0$$

which is the *pendulum equation.*

Alas, there is no solution to this equation, simple though it may appear. Not even the infinite-series techniques in the previous chapter will work for this equation. That sounds rather discouraging, yet there is a relatively simple trick we can employ to at least arrive at an approximate solution.

Going back to our sine-curve plot in Chapter 21, we see that for small values of x (typically between -0.1 and 0.1 radians), $\sin x$ is basically equal to x. Indeed, at 0.1 radians, the sine value is off by less than 0.02 percent. So, for small angles, we can rewrite the pendulum equation as

$$\frac{d^2x}{dt^2} + \frac{g}{l}x = 0$$

or

$$\frac{d^2x}{dt^2} = -\frac{g}{l}x$$

which is a carbon-copy of the SHO equation for the perfect spring examined in the previous chapter. Its solution is exactly the same save for the constants, which will depend on g and l rather than the spring constant k and bob mass m. As was the case with the spring, the pendulum, even as it swings through a small angle, will encounter air resistance; due to the small travel distance of the bob, however, this resistance will be negligible.

Everyone has seen a pendulum with a small angular swing; it's found in every grandfather's clock. This is why the equation

$$\frac{d^2x}{dt^2} = -\frac{g}{l}x$$

is sometimes called the *grandfather's clock equation*. The negligible air resistance enables the grandfather's clock pendulum to swing back and forth for a very long period of time, perhaps months or even years, if the pendulum arm and bob are constructed and calibrated carefully and accurately.

At this point, it's time to wrap things up. A lot of information was presented in this book, and I hope I put it out in a way that was interesting, even entertaining—but most of all, in a way that piqued your interest in mathematics. You can think of this book as a guide, maybe a quick reference; it wasn't intended as an in-depth, exhaustive compendium of every mathematical concept, idea and discovery that ever existed. I would encourage you to do a lot of exploration on your own, especially online. There are myriad Web sites that deal with mathematical concepts; a favorite of mine is the Math Warehouse (http://www.mathwarehouse.com). This has interactive and animated demonstrations of mathematics that, along with this book, can really give you a deep understanding of math beyond just the rote memorization that is all too often used in teaching math.

So good luck, take care, and remember—make math your friend, and you'll have a friend for life!

Printed in the United States
By Bookmasters